LEADING YOUR BUSINESS TO THE NEXT LEVEL

LEADING YOUR BUSINESS
TO THE NEXT LEVEL

The Six Core Disciplines of
Sustained Profitable Growth

Rodney Page and Pete Tosh

Westport, Connecticut
London

HD
2746
.P34
2005

Library of Congress Cataloging-in-Publication Data

Page, Rodney, 1947-
   Leading your business to the next level : the six core disciplines of
sustained profitable growth / Rodney Page and Pete Tosh.
      p.   cm.
   Includes bibliographical references and index.
   ISBN 0-275-98749-3 (alk. paper)
   1. Corporations–Growth.   2. Success in business.   3. Organizational
effectiveness.   4. Industrial management.   5. Strategic planning.   I. Tosh,
Pete, 1944–   II. Title.
   HD2746.P34 2005
   658.4'092–dc22   2005009814

British Library Cataloguing in Publication Data is available.

Library of Congress Catalog Card Number: 2005009814
ISBN: 0-275-98749-3

First published in 2005

Praeger Publishers, 88 Post Road West, Westport, CT 06881
An imprint of Greenwood Publishing Group, Inc.
www.praeger.com

Printed in the United States of America

The paper used in this book complies with the
Permanent Paper Standard issued by the National
Information Standards Organization (Z39.48-1984).

10 9 8 7 6 5 4 3 2 1

CONTENTS

ACKNOWLEDGMENTS

We would like to thank all the individuals we have been fortunate enough to work with over the last thirty-five years. The optimistic tone of this book is founded in the firm belief that the huge majority of the business leaders of this country and their employees are hard-working people who want to improve their and their organizations' performance. That assumption made our task of writing this book an energizing experience. Offering guidance and suggestions to readers who want to make themselves and their companies more successful was a gratifying and fulfilling exercise for the authors.

This book would not have been possible if not for Stan Wakefield and our editor at Praeger, Nick Philipson. Without their enthusiastic and positive support, this book would never have been published. Their optimism, patience, and professional guidance have made them a joy to deal with.

Last, we are tremendously grateful for the support of our families and friends, whose first reaction to the concept of authoring a book could easily have been skepticism . . . but it wasn't. It was the opposite. Without their continuing support and patience, this book would have remained just a concept.

INTRODUCTION

Our sixty-five-plus years (Wow, has it been that many?) working for and with growth companies have allowed us to observe and participate in successful and some not-so-successful enterprises. The single common characteristic of those that were able to sustain profitable growth was that they simply did not collapse under the weight of their success.

Research and observation identify many factors critical for companies to sustain growth, one of the most common being a lack of sufficient capital to finance surging growth. This is especially true of successful entrepreneurial firms that survive start-up and experience an early growth surge. We agree with the vital role adequate capital plays in ongoing success, but lack of capital is the devil everyone is familiar with. And, there is no lack of attention paid to it in today's business press.

But what about the demons we may not be familiar with, demons that lurk within every company and are primed to pounce if given the slightest opportunity?

There's a certain sad irony in situations where a company has developed a product or service that is in high demand in the marketplace, identified a successful niche, has the ability to sell at a very high volume, and yet cannot sustain profitable growth. What makes ongoing success so difficult to achieve? Why, in fact, does success lead to failure? How can self-inflicted wounds be more severe than those caused by a finicky marketplace or aggressive competitors?

The authors posit that an organization's inability to acknowledge and actively master the Six Core Growth Disciplines is a primary reason why so many "shooting stars" fizzle out just as quickly as they brilliantly burst onto the scene.

We begin the book with a chapter entitled "Growth and Its Challenges." Specifically targeted to management of early growth companies, it is a frank and sometimes frightening look at the litany of challenges, complexities, and urgencies facing rapidly growing organizations. Consider it a primer and early warning system, observations of the strategic, operational, cultural, and personal tribulations brought on by rapid growth.

This chapter is of particular relevance to companies experiencing or about to experience early growth. Frankly, the survivability of such companies is tenuous at best at this point. The ability of these companies' managers to recognize and successfully cope with the harsh realities they face is essential to survival. Once these problems are acknowledged and dealt with, management is in a position to refine its practices and move forward toward mastery of the Six Core Disciplines.

THE SIX CORE GROWTH DISCIPLINES

Discipline: "mental self-control used in directing or changing behavior"

So, that's the definition from the dictionary. What does it mean in the context of growth? The operative word in the definition is "self-control." The inference is that we know what we should be doing; we must insure that we just do it. No problem! The definition certainly applies to the Six Core Growth Disciplines. They're not terribly complex; they're not exercises in radical new management theory; they're not an unveiling of previously undiscovered "secrets of success."

You will recognize them immediately. They have to do with such novel concepts as keeping customers, good planning, effective execution and leadership, people, and profitability. Not much new here . . . or is there?

The "new" presented here is the relationship between accepted, sound management practices and the ability of companies to sustain profitable growth. And, that relationship is rather critical: Profitable growth can simply not be sustained without mastery of these disciplines. It's that simple.

Can an organization survive and grow by mastering just one or a few of the disciplines? It depends.

Are there lost opportunities for profitable growth if all the disciplines are not mastered? Absolutely.

Will mastery of all the disciplines insure sustained profitable growth? No, but the odds for success increase dramatically.

Is sustained, profitable growth impossible if all Six Core Growth Disciplines are absent? Absolutely, and you can take that to the bank; but you will have little else to take.

DISCIPLINE #1: SUSTAINING GROWTH THROUGH ENHANCED CUSTOMER LOYALTY

"You can't grow if you're shrinking!"

We owe that quote to an unknown author whose work we read many years ago. Shame we didn't think of it. We have seen several examples of rapidly growing companies brought to their knees by the erosion of their existing customer base. More "rocket science": For every customer you lose, you have to acquire another one just to be back where you started. (Well, almost, not counting customer acquisition costs.)

Data and examples abound. It costs five times more to acquire a customer than to keep one. Profits from existing customers are consistently higher than from new ones. It goes on and on, but somehow, many companies cannot bring themselves to 1) fully appreciate the value of their existing customers, and, 2) if they are appreciated, implement the processes and business rules that will increase customer loyalty.

The "Basics"

- Customers remain loyal when their expectations are met or exceeded.
- You must know your customers' expectations.
- Your company's strategies, goals, and objectives must be supportive of meeting customers' expectations.
- Your company's practices for customer-contact employees must be aligned with and in support of customers' expectations, and
- Customer-contact employees must be equipped with the tools and supported by management practices that are geared to meeting customer expectations.

The Bottom Line

Effective strategies and processes have a tangible impact on the company's bottom line. It's been proven time and time again that innovative hiring/development and process/development efforts more than pay for themselves in terms of improved customer service, greater customer loyalty, and, ultimately, improved profitability.

DISCIPLINE #2: DYNAMIC PLANNING AND BUDGETING

During rapid growth, conventional planning and budgeting models are rendered obsolete due to the high rate of change. Planning assumptions and the strategies that flow from them are often outdated by the time the planning documents and spreadsheets are printed; if not then, certainly within the next quarter or two.

How does a successful growth company, in the midst of dealing with these massive day-to-day challenges, incorporate the impact of the ever-changing environment and the ever-changing company itself into its plans? The senior management team does not have the luxury to be, nor does it want to be, in a planning mode constantly.

And, the budget must be inexorably linked to the business plan. So it must also be modified to support revised plans as well as the "actuals" as they are reported.

A growth company must effectively deal with these associated changes by installing flexible planning and budgeting tools. Conventional models simply aren't well suited to the dynamic world of fast-paced growth.

Companies must get the "baseline" right, effectively deal with the inevitable dynamics that exist in the marketplace and within the company, and link the plans and budgets to the desired behaviors of the employees.

DISCIPLINE #3: EXECUTING THE BUSINESS PLAN

As they say, 90 percent is in the execution. Great plans are meaningless without effective execution. Dynamic planning will insure that meaningful strategies are in place, but planning doesn't occur everyday—tactical execution does.

Senior management makes dozens of decisions every day. So does everyone else in the organization. In the rapidly changing environment of a growth company, how can management insure that those decisions, the follow-through, and its employees' behaviors are aligned with the company's strategies and plans?

In a growth company, the risk of making both tactical and strategic decisions that do not support the company's stated plans is significant. A senior director hired last month is thrust into a highly responsible job and asked to make decisions without having the company background that he and the senior team would desire.

Major and mundane decisions are made daily. Not everyone in the company possesses the intuitive knowledge of the plan that the senior team members have. One morning the "wheels come off," and, in retrospect, a bad decision was made by someone who simply didn't know better.

Some things are executed effectively, some aren't. Certain initiatives exceed management's expectations while others fail miserably. Lessons can and must be learned from both successes and failures.

As growth continues and the company matures, more and more must be done through others. Organizations grow, as do their management layers. Senior management's ability to delegate effectively takes on a heightened level of importance. Likewise does the insight and perseverance to create those processes that bring uniformity and efficiency. But, the path between chaos and good bureaucracy is very narrow.

DISCIPLINE #4: MAXIMIZING SENIOR LEADERSHIP EFFECTIVENESS

Ah, leadership, the great intangible that is so important.

An assumption evident throughout the book is the existence of an ever-changing environment that growth companies face and must successfully contend with in order to sustain growth and not be overwhelmed by it. Nowhere is that more critical than with the leaders of the company.

The senior management team of a growth company is constantly changing, in ways over and above the obvious. The makeup of the team changes as the company grows. Some founders and original executives will likely leave the firm. New executives are brought in. There will be promotions from within.

Not so obvious are the mandatory changes in the individuals themselves. Assignments and responsibilities are constantly changing. It is very unlikely that the duties of executives will be the same at the end of the year as they were at the beginning, even though job titles may remain the same. The members of the senior team are continually evolving, growing and maturing as individuals, as necessitated by the changes in their jobs and in the company itself.

Additionally, the senior management team is faced with evolving and more complex delegation challenges...getting things done through others, while the "others" are also growing by leaps and bounds. The moral compass must remain true, and growing functional responsibilities and priorities must be balanced against those of the company as a whole.

And, the senior team must function effectively as a team in the truest and most meaningful sense of the word. Skills, experiences, personalities, egos, and individual priorities must be meshed and re-meshed continually to insure that the effectiveness of the whole truly exceeds that of the sum of its individuals.

Anything less is, frankly, unacceptable and will prevent the organization from realizing its full potential.

DISCIPLINE #5: CHANGING EMPHASIS FROM SALES/REVENUE TO MARGIN/PROFIT

Companies moving out of the entrepreneurial stage into early growth are commonly very focused on sales and revenue. It is likely that sales is one of the largest, if not the dominant, functions in the enterprise. Customers and revenue are all important, and rightfully so . . . cash flow is paramount.

However, too much growth and/or growth of the wrong kind poses extremely serious challenges for rapidly growing companies. Sales practices and guidelines were likely loosely structured, fostering an "any customer is a good customer" attitude. Prices may have fallen as the company battled for a foothold in the market. Sales increased, but the company may be engaging in nonsustainable growth. The scenario above can lead to unacceptable gross margins. The sales volume created by aggressive pricing can also lead to an overload of the company's product/service delivery capabilities, a reduction in the quality of customer support and service, and a strain on the firm's administrative and back office systems.

The scenario described above is not unique to start-up firms. The allure of sales and revenue has a way of creeping into companies of any size and at any stage of maturity. The very thought that certain customers or market segments are undesirable is generally counter-intuitive, and this is most certainly so to sales executives if their only yardstick of success is revenue.

However, research and experience clearly indicate that not all customers are desirable:

- The *Harvard Business Review* estimates that, on average, 15 percent of all customers are unprofitable.
- Larry Selden and Geoffrey Colvin in their book *Angel Customers & Demon Customers* estimate that, in most industries, the best 20 percent

of customers account for 150 percent of profits; the worst 20 percent typically lose money equal to 75 percent of profits.[1]

- And, a medium-size service firm found that the highest-revenue customers were the least profitable . . . in fact, they were not profitable at all!

Not only are some customers and segments likely not profitable, such is the case with products. In this era of hyper–product specialization and multiple and complex products and product lines, the odds that all will be profitable are rather low. Thomas K. Brown writing in the *Bank Director* magazine estimates that for a typical bank, the top 10 percent most profitable bank products generate 70 percent of overall profits. Conversely, the bottom 80 percent contribute less than 1 percent of profits.[2] Lots of revenue and lots of products do not necessarily translate into lots of profit.

DISCIPLINE #6: POSITIONING HR MANAGEMENT AS A STRATEGIC ADVANTAGE

When the company was young, it is likely that senior management played an active role in recruiting the best associates. Expertise was readily available to the new employees, and this mentoring and on-the-job development served the company well. However, growth requires the continual influx of new employees in greater and greater numbers, and the former "word of mouth development" simply doesn't work anymore. It is likely that the "people function" of the business (aka human resources) was late developing. And though people are the heart of any company, recruiting, retention, and development of the ever-growing employee body, from senior executives to the associates, may not have received the critical attention it deserves.

We believe that a growing company's human resources capabilities and its sophistication can and should provide a strategic advantage over its competitors. The right employees with the right skills and motivation available at the right time will sustain growth. However, if the "people function" is an afterthought, a critical strategic edge is lost, and otherwise achievable opportunities will not be realized.

SUMMARY

So, what do we have here?

In the broadest sense, companies must clearly perceive and exercise the discipline (self-control) to realize that:

- Keeping good customers is a financial "winner" by any measure, and management must develop and implement those initiatives required to make sure they don't leave.
- Static planning and budgeting regimens are not compatible with the dynamics of a growth environment, and these processes must be continually modified in keeping with the world in which they exist.
- The best planning is meaningless without high-quality execution, and the company must develop management practices to insure that execution is always consistent with the goals of the organization.
- Effective leadership is difficult in any environment, but even more so during rapid growth and change, and management must enthusiastically embrace the evolving requirements of an effective leadership team.
- Not all customers and products contribute equally to the enterprise's profitability, and the company must conduct the necessary analysis and make the necessary decisions that seem so counter to conventional wisdom.
- The human resource function is more than a necessary overhead, and must be fully integrated into the organization's business and strategic planning.

SMALL AND LARGE COMPANIES

No matter the size and longevity of an organization, it is susceptible to the internal "demons" described earlier. Companies and their departments become complacent. Old ways of doing things that used to work become ingrained and almost unchallengeable. Companies can get "fat and lazy" both in terms of marketplace position and creative agility.

Therefore, no matter the size and age of the enterprise, and no matter if at some time in the past some or all of the Six Core Growth Disciplines had been mastered, if that mastery has been lost, it must be resurrected. No company, regardless of its size and historical resilience, can expect to continue to sustain profitable growth in the future if these "demons" raise their ugly heads.

OUR READERS

Leading Your Business to the Next Level: The Six Core Disciplines of Sustained Profitable Growth is written *to* the senior management of companies that are leaving the start-up phase and moving through an early growth stage; but it is also written *for* executives and managers of companies of all sizes and in all stages of corporate maturity.

With that in mind, this book asks you to put yourself in the role of a senior manager in that early-stage growth company. For some of you, that's exactly where you are.

For those of you in more mature companies, allow the book to stimulate retrospection of critical fundamentals that likely led your company to its current level of success, but may have become diminished over time and are inhibiting the company from reaching its full potential.

For you start-up entrepreneurs, this book will act as a guide for problem preemption. It will let you know what's coming over the next few hills and provide a plan for developing management practices that you won't have to overhaul later. You're in the enviable position of creating, not correcting.

For all of you, read and enjoy.

Chapter 1

GROWTH AND ITS CHALLENGES

CONGRATULATIONS, YOU'RE GROWING

And, the congratulations are fully warranted! However, both the positives and negatives of growth must be acknowledged. The positives are obvious: Revenues are going up, day-to-day survival is a thing of the past. The negatives may be more subtle. As an astute executive, you intuitively know that things are changing, but do you know just how much?

This chapter is intended to provide a few moments for introspection and reflection. It's likely that you will be reading this outside the office; at home, on vacation, on a plane. The chapter provides more questions than answers simply because the answers originate in you, not the authors. Many of the issues and questions raised are at the visceral level: the core of what your company is, what you are, and what you want the company to become. Consider them as thought-provokers to challenge your mind and your heart as you continue your quest of sustained, profitable growth.

The Thrill of It All

You are part of a management team experiencing one of the most exhilarating thrills in the world of business: managing a company that is successful and growing. The personal satisfaction, challenges, and rewards that are part of this experience are huge. You are part of a thriving enterprise that is now, or has the potential to become, a significant player in your industry. The hopes and dreams that were a twinkle in your eye not too long ago are being fulfilled, and you have a reasonable chance of exceeding your wildest expectations. The management team's accomplishments cannot be minimized. The pride you all feel is real and well deserved.

But with the company's rapid growth come challenges that are unique, challenges not faced in the entrepreneurial phase or by large, established corporations. The growing organization faces obstacles created by its very success: physical expansion, new and challenging relationships (with vendors, customers, government agencies), lessons learned the hard way, encounters with individuals who may not have the enterprise's best interests at heart. It's not unlike raising a child moving from infancy, through early adolescence, through the teenage years to early adulthood, and, finally, to maturity. Though the "hormone factor" isn't present, the stress and turmoil experienced in managing a growing company is certainly analogous to parenting.

Growing up is tough for people and companies, but the outcome is highly desirable in both cases. As a parent or member of the management team, the personal and professional fulfillment of watching children and companies grow and blossom is hard to match.

Growth Is Good!

That is something to remember as you confront and manage the ups and downs of a growing company. The old adage "If you're not growing, you're dying" is as true as it ever was. Companies, like organisms, must grow and not atrophy. The security and comforts of the status quo are not an option for the management team, investors, or employees.

In his book *Rising Stars and Fast Fades*, W. Keith Schilit points out some interesting statistics:

- Most businesses that file for bankruptcy have less than a hundred employees.
- Survival rates double for companies that have grown.
- Companies that have grown the most successfully have survival rates of over 80 percent.
- Companies need at least $500,000 in revenue to escape what he calls the "zone of vulnerability."
- Chances of survival and prosperity increase dramatically when annual sales exceed $1 million.[1]

To restate the obvious, no matter how ambitious your growth aspirations, they must exist. If the team is content with building and managing a modest and comfortable business and does not want to grow the company, if it doesn't want to maximize the wealth of the owners, this book is not for you.

You can remain small and stable and avoid the headaches, stress, and turmoil of high growth, but you may not be able to survive. And, it wouldn't be near as much fun.

You're Growing: Do You Deserve It?

Your company is either growing or you anticipate it doing so, or you would not be reading this book. In either case, the current or anticipated reality is that you are acquiring more customers or soon will. Therefore, early in this text, we present the first of many self-assessment questions posed in this book: Do you deserve the success you're experiencing? Are you lucky or good?

Not to minimize efforts that led to early success, the team should critically analyze the reasons for it and determine, frankly, how much they had to do with it. More important, are the factors that led to this growth sustainable over time? And, will the growth be profitable? Consider the following factors:

A Unique Product Other than a patentable product, process, or service, are you benefiting from uniqueness that competitors are not able to replicate in the marketplace? How long will you be the only company offering the product? What will the competitors' responses be, and how well are you equipped to deal with them?

A Rising Tide Did you benefit from a general upturn in the economy or a spurt in a certain segment? Was the timing of the introduction of the product fortuitous? Is everyone in the "space" successful? When will the tide go out?

Regulatory/Legislative Action Were "rules" changed by the government that provided a windfall of opportunity? Are the changes permanent? What will happen if the "rules" are changed again and become disadvantageous to the company?

A Competitor's Misfortune/Mistakes Did someone else's problem lead to your success? Will they correct the problem, and when will they do it? What happens if and when they do?

A Few "Bluebirds" Flew Over Did a relatively small number of sales contribute to the majority of your success? How long will you have these accounts? What could you do to replace them?

Again, any "good luck" may well have been a result of insightful product development, astute monitoring of the regulatory environment, and great sales efforts. However, the major question is whether the company proactively created and executed initiatives that will insure ongoing growth and make it independent of external, uncontrollable conditions.

- Was it consciously or unconsciously beginning to master the Six Core Disciplines?
- Did the company's competencies lead directly to its prosperity, and will those abilities enable the company to maintain its early success?
- Is the company mindful of how important it is to keep its customers?
- Do the company's planning processes identify clear strategies that provide flexibility to effectively deal with the ever-changing variables inherent in a high-growth environment?
- What is the company's ability to execute the plan?
- Is the management team learning and evolving at the rate a high-growth company demands? Does it interact and communicate effectively?
- Is the company selling the right products to the right customers? Has past growth been profitable?
- Is the company capable of acquiring, developing, and retaining the key element of successful growth: competent and motivated employees?

So, you're growing, and that's the good news. The euphoria, ego-stroking, and potential for wealth creation are positive and powerful motivators. However, they must be balanced with the recognition of the difficult challenges that accompany growth. It's not easy, nor is there any "Midas touch."

There will be milestones of success, but a company's ability to successfully manage its way through high-growth times is not a destination; rather, it is a journey, a journey that never really ends but can lead to levels of wealth and professional satisfaction found in few other business endeavors.

GUT-CHECK: DO YOU REALLY WANT TO MOVE INTO THE BIG TIME?

The purpose of this book is not to dissuade management teams from pursuing rapid growth. In fact, it's quite the contrary. However, a realistic presentation of issues that must be successfully addressed and the skills that must evolve lay the groundwork for later observations and recommendations.

Depending on your company and its location on the growth trajectory chart, you will identify with the issues identified in this chapter. The management team is faced with a constantly evolving array of tasks and competency requirements. Simple awareness will forewarn the senior management team of these changes.

More important, the team must be completely committed to exerting the effort it will take to adequately prepare themselves for what awaits them. The four listed requirements are independent, but presented in a logical sequence. As usual, senior management effectiveness is at the top of the list, with the ability to deliver quality products and services as the eventual output.

Overarching Requirements of Management

Redefinition of Senior Management Roles The requisite competencies, management skills, and organizational abilities of the senior management team are in constant flux. Job responsibilities evolve; old duties become obsolete as new ones emerge. The collaborative management of start-up changes as discrete business functions and departments evolve. The old dogs must constantly learn new tricks.

Speed and Urgency Growth companies face an environment that demands an ever-increasing pace. Issues that must be managed at any given time grow exponentially, and so does their complexity. Sheer size complicates matters: more people, more customers, more departments—all of these tax management and infrastructure. Decision-making has more import and more moving parts. And, decisions must be made ever more swiftly.

Process Development The natural consequence of growth is the requirement to "get organized." The move from a few employees making intuitive decisions about everything to standardization is arduous. And, moving from the chaos of start-up to a process orientation that is not bureaucratically stifling is a major challenge.

Product Delivery Scalability The ability to insure product delivery, high quality, and customer support must keep up with sales increases. Production/delivery capabilities must match sales growth; in fact, they must stay ahead. Failure of them to do so has led to the ruin of many high-growth companies and continues to afflict others today.

Attitude and Perspective

The management team also deals with "softer" issues no less compelling and critical. They concern the inevitable changes in the company, the way it conducts business, and how it views itself. The camaraderie, shared values, and informal communications that were characteristics of the company early on change. The change can and should be positive. But, it may shock and dismay members of the team and other employees. The simple fact remains: Life in the company will never be the same.

At the risk of overgeneralization, the following management perspectives are found all too often in growth firms. They all, in one way or another, are focused on the past, perhaps on at a time when the team was in a "comfort zone." Emphasis on the past will likely not bring success in the future.

"We used to do it this way and that way" The importance of senior management's wholehearted endorsement of change required for growth cannot be overstated. The early success that brought the company out of start-up required a distinct set of management skills and capabilities. Some continue to be valid; others aren't and must be modified or replaced. Looking back instills a sense of pride and is the stuff of company legend. Looking forward is the stuff of which wealth is built.

"We don't do it that way." The team must think long and hard before it utters this statement. Sticking to core cultural values must continue, but everything else is open to fresh and pointed reevaluation. Maybe you didn't "do it that way" a year ago or a month ago, but you need to do it differently now. The variables are constantly changing, and new ones will be added. Companies that don't learn to "do it a different way" often find themselves not able to do it at all.

"I'll just do it myself." Perhaps this was appropriate in the early days when there was no one else to do it. The senior team must master the skills of getting things done through others. Effective delegation is critical as management changes with the company. The inability to shed inappropriate tasks wastes precious time and energy, and diverts attention from new challenges.

"We're pretty good if we made it this far." The natural trepidation and hyperurgency of start-up paid off in early success. Overconfidence was not a threat when doubt existed about making payroll and wondering where the next customer was going to come from.

Early success provided breathing room, a little cash in the bank, and confidence that survival is possible. However, early success does not insure long-term viability of the firm nor necessarily guarantee that it will reach its potential. Confidence has been rightfully gained. Overconfidence would be a severe misinterpretation of early success.

"Our employees have fared quite well on their own up until now." Yes, they probably have. Early hires were made by the executives. Staffing needs were minimal, and the company was very selective in hiring new members of the "family." Significant growth means more employees. Though the hiring goal may be to attract more people like the "veterans," it is difficult. Management's attention to employee development requires discipline, resources, and commitment.

Additional Issues You Can Look Forward To

- Production/support is not keeping up with demand—or, there is too much production/support overhead for the current sales volume.
- New product development is always behind schedule.
- The original building is too small.
- Legal and regulatory issues; requirements and edicts you never imagined suddenly appear.
- Employee communications that were once so simple now seem so complex.
- You don't have enough people and customer service suffers; you have too many and profitability suffers.
- The personalized and attentive customer service once provided now seems impossible.
- The employee "family" (now extended) doesn't seem to get along as well as it used to.
- Costs creep up despite efforts to keep things "lean and mean."
- Cost-cutting becomes necessary, but there seems to be no "fat."
- Competitors who could have cared less about your company begin to pay attention.
- Once valid assumptions aren't anymore.
- The gross margin that has been solid begins to deteriorate.
- Leadership was involuntary; it now requires proactive effort.
- It's a constant struggle to develop proper business controls and processes without creating a bureaucracy.
- Unionization rears its head.

- Once valuable data is now not telling you what you need to know.
- Nobody seems to have enough time.
- Not everyone who was with the company from the start can "cut it" now.
- Some employees are beginning to play loose with facts and numbers, behaviors counter to what you thought the company's ethics were all about.
- The company's departments grow and mature; the old collaborative teamwork gives way to "turf" battles and political jockeying.
- You're on an airplane more than ever; the family wants to know when the incessant travel will end.
- Somebody sues you.
- And, cash is as big a problem as ever, except now the numbers are bigger.

The chapter title posed the question: Do you really want to move to the big time? If the answer is yes, you must lead the company through growth and its challenges. The headaches and heartaches are inevitable, but the thrill of guiding a living and ever-changing organism (the company and the people in it) through it all is exhilarating.

Don't let the list discourage you. Those challenges and others will be successfully confronted if you know they're coming and maintain the will to face them.

IS THE GROWTH SUSTAINABLE?

Growth is good. However, growth that is not sustainable or profitable may prove as fatal as no growth at all. Consider, for example, the case of a technology company that experienced tremendous double-digit growth for three years running. The business plan was solid and a lucrative niche was identified. The company approached $30 million in annual revenue at its peak. That was three years ago . . . but the company is now out of business.

Though several factors contributed to the company's demise, the major villain was the company's inability to provide the level of customer support it once had when it was smaller. This company actually grew itself to death.

The previous section identified a list of problems and issues that management can expect to encounter. It is a reasonable assessment of what is expected of senior management in order to move the company forward. Now, the requirements needed in order to sustain growth must be considered.

Growth versus Sustainable and Profitable Growth

Compared to sustained profitable growth, plain old growth is relatively easy to achieve. It's simply a matter of maximizing sales volume until the company encounters one or more of the following:

- You run out of cash.
- The back office breaks down.
- Customer service deteriorates.
- You can't bill your customers.
- You can't hire enough people.
- Etc., etc., etc.

How often have we heard, "Nothing happens until somebody sells something." There should be a follow-up adage: "Not much is going to happen if somebody sells too much."

Many firms view growth overly simplistically. It is viewed as an orderly, linear process where the company incrementally increases the number of tasks it has always conducted commensurate with the increased sales volume and number of customers:

- Sell more.
- Produce/deliver more product/service.
- Send out more bills.
- Hire more people for customer service.
- Collect more money.

Regrettably, it isn't that simple. Growth is not a linear, evenly proportioned process. Sustained profitable growth requires far more than a company just doing more of what it has been doing; it requires continual evolution of existing competencies and capabilities, and the development of new ones.

Attributes of Sustained Profitable Growth

So, what are the "biggies"? Each of these and others will be discussed in more detail later. Though some of the "biggies" are incorporated into the Six Core Disciplines, these attributes should be viewed as prerequisites, or the foundation stone on which to master the disciplines.

They include some that are internal to and controllable by the company; others are more external. Some are "soft"; some are "hard." A common thread connecting all of them is that the complete absence of any one will negatively impact your quest for sustained profitable growth.

Core Ethics The company's ethical underpinnings coupled with unwavering consistency in the application of those principles provide the social foundation for the company's growth. Everyone responds best to the pressure and uncertainty to come if they are confident that the company and its senior management team are trustworthy.

A Knowledgeable and Supportive Board Boards are composed of a variety of members who have different backgrounds and levels of business savvy. Second and third-round financing often alters the board's makeup and its collective business sophistication. The board should actively counsel with senior management, and the executives should welcome and embrace this valuable input.

The Management Team's Capabilities The senior executives' responsibilities and the shareholders' and employees' expectations increase dramatically with growth. Team members must be honest with themselves and the board to insure that the right people with the right talent are in the right place.

Middle Management The company's senior management team finds itself removed from the day-to-day routine of running the company's operations. They are refocusing their time and energy on strategic challenges. Middle management must have the knowledge and people skills to relieve executives of these tactical responsibilities.

Financing Growth requires capital and lots of it. Positive cash flow alone does not finance the requirements of a high-growth company. The management team must identify sources of capital and initiate steps to acquire that capital long before they need it.

The Players in the Space A fragmented market with many companies sharing small percentages of market share offers growth opportunities. Conversely, industries that have a high market share held by a few dominant competitors will make sustained growth more difficult.

Uniqueness: The Value Proposition The company must offer the market real and/or perceived value not currently offered by the competition. Unless the company offers something unique, it will be just another of many similar providers delivering a homogeneous product or service.

Market/Product Viability A growth market/product enhances sustainability. The clichés describe the concept well: "A rising tide raises all boats"; "The buggy whip industry was doomed with the invention of the automobile." A declining economy or market, regulatory/policy uncertainty, or dependence on a product/service where technological obsolescence is lurking in the wings—none are characteristics of high-growth companies.

Sales Channels Tried and tested sales channels enhance the firm's ability to grow. Reactive experimentation or rushed deployment of unfamiliar and unproven channels does not produce the desired increases in sales volume.

People Development Employee acquisition and development processes must run smoothly before being put to the real test. Haphazard and unsophisticated human resource processes will not provide the required qualified new employees.

Leveraging Your Competencies Growth requires the company to venture into new markets, develop new products, and initiate entire new business plans. Such changes require radically different competencies when compared to those currently existing.

Growth and sustained profitable growth are very different. Has your company positioned itself to enter the intense world of sustaining profitable growth? Complete the following self-assessment for an indication. Be honest. Discovering weaknesses in your company here could save you a lot of heartburn in the future.

SUSTAINABLE GROWTH SELF-ASSESSMENT

1 = Strongly Disagree
2 = Somewhat Disagree
3 = N/A; Don't Know
4 = Somewhat Agree
5 = Strongly Agree

Add up the points.
Your company's positioning for significant growth:

113–125	Extremely well prepared
100–112	Reasonably well prepared
88–99	Possesses some of the prerequisites
75–87	Possesses a few of the prerequisites
< 75	Sustainable growth will be difficult

Table 1.1 Sustainable Growth Self-Assessment

	1	2	3	4	5
The company knows who its customers are, where they are located, what they buy, how much they buy, and what industries they are in.					
The company knows why its customers buy its products.					
The company knows who its competitors are, their products and pricing, their strategies and tactics, and their strengths and weaknesses.					
Management has confidence in the company's strategic/business plan; all key members of the team understand the plan and are committed to it.					
The company has certain uniqueness in the marketplace that is captured in its value proposition; everyone in the company is familiar with the value proposition.					
The company has well-defined goals and objectives, and all the key players know what they are and if the company is achieving them.					
The company's metrics and key indicators provide an accurate picture of how well the company performed and provides insight into predicting how well it will do in the future.					
The company's middle management team is fully in place and capable of running the company's day-to-day operations.					
Technology is in place that automates a significant portion of the company's internal and customer support processes.					
Basic policies and procedures are in place that address the significant functions and operations of the business; sophisticated policies and procedures are in place to address financial, legal, and regulatory activities.					
The company is in a high-growth market or market segment.					
The company's existing and planned products are in demand and are not likely to be replaced by new technology or substitute products.					
The political/regulatory environment poses no significant threats to the business plan.					

Table 1.1 (*Continued*)

	1	2	3	4	5
The company's production/delivery processes and systems are scalable and within the capacity of the business plan to support.					
Human resources are available to support growth.					
Employee orientation and training programs are in place to develop the skill and knowledge requirements of the expanding employee body.					
The company's facilities and telecommunications/ information technology infrastructure are adequate to support growth.					
Market share is fragmented among many small and medium-size firms and not dominated by one or a few dominant player(s).					
The company's sales channels are mature and capable of achieving ever-increasing objectives.					
The company's management team has demonstrated capabilities in leading a high-growth company.					
The company has identified equity/debt to finance the growth.					
The company's board is capable of providing competent and meaningful insight and guidance to senior management and is willing to do so.					
The company's growth plans utilize existing knowledge and competencies and do not require extensive "new learning."					
The management team is totally committed to the growth plan.					
The company's ethics clearly provide the "moral compass" for how business will be conducted.					

YOUR COMPANY'S STAGE OF GROWTH

Research for this book uncovered many definitions of the "growth stages of businesses." Some are based on employee count, some on annual revenue. Still others are based on combinations of other quantitative and qualitative indicators. The common denominator for all the "stage" or "phase" theories is that companies develop distinctly different and changing characteristics as they grow. No matter how one defines the stages, companies exhibit common behaviors and face common challenges. And, the responses to those challenges generally tend to be fairly similar among companies.

Stage discussions are similar to horoscope readings. Whatever your sign, there are enough broad descriptors so almost any individual will find something relative. Stage descriptions contain enough generalizations so any company can find those characteristics in most any stage, particularly if the characteristics are positive.

Cynicism aside, the relevance of stages centers on awareness and preparedness. Though there are no perfect definitions of stages, they do provide a useful tool in calibrating just where a company is and what it can anticipate in the future. Like any consultants worth their salt, we would be remiss if we did not develop our own version of the growth stages of a business. So, here they are.

Self-Assessment: Where Is Your Company?

Take a few minutes to review the descriptors. You will probably find characteristics of several stages that apply to your company. Simply check those that describe your current environment as an informal categorization of where your company stands today.

Entrepreneurial

- Informality and doing the expedient characterize operations. Effective "fire fighting" is a core strategy and chaos is the norm.
- Initial funding (what there may be of it) likely comes from founders and individual investors.
- The founders do everything; the more general their business backgrounds and experiences, the better.
- Decision-making is intuitive. If management's business instincts are astute, the "if it feels good do it" approach works.
- Almost any customer is a good customer. There is minimal if any segmentation of the market.
- The product portfolio is limited. Alterations or new product development are usually driven by specific customer demands.
- There may be a business plan in place, but it evolves tactically every day. The investors required "a plan," but it is likely not directly driving business activities.
- Selling is probably the key function in the business. Acquiring customers is absolutely critical. There is minimal if any presence of a formal marketing function.
- Legal and financial-related issues receive some formal "process" attention. Most other activities are unstructured.

- Short term focus: Making next week's payroll is of paramount importance.

Early Growth Spurt

- The company has moderate success in the marketplace. A niche has evolved and a value proposition emerges that is accepted by certain segments of the market.
- A growing need for additional capital becomes evident. Marketplace success begins to attract the interest of additional investors and lenders.
- A management hierarchy begins to take shape. Supervisors and managers are appointed to begin to relieve senior management of some hands-on daily responsibilities.
- The increased volume crystallizes the requirement for process development. These may be manual initially, but the need for automation becomes more and more clear.
- The competition begins to take notice of the company. Operating below the radar is no longer possible, and competitors begin to respond to the company's success.
- The product portfolio begins to grow; however, the driver is no longer disjointed customer demands. Product development begins to take on a more formal and structured form based on anticipated demands and new, broader opportunities.
- Reactive management begins to give way to more orderly decision-making. The complexities of the business have reached the point where data must be acquired and analysis undertaken.
- Financial and key operating metrics begin to replace the less formal "Can we make it another month?" emphasis of start-up.
- Sales success begins to overload the capabilities of the company's infrastructure. Awareness of the necessity to match fulfillment and support capabilities with sales volume begins to set in.
- Growth reveals gaps in the company's talent and competencies. Critical personnel are recruited frantically, and some of the hiring decisions prove faulty due to lack of a formal process.

Adolescence

- The company is officially "successful." Though, like a teenager, it may have the physical size of an adult, it is not fully mature.
- New employees must be hired by the score. The supply of "good" people is not available to meet requirements, and the company must invest in extensive orientation, training, and development efforts.
- The need for formal process development is fully recognized. Resources are dedicated to formalizing the business, to the distress of many employees who whine about the company's growing bureaucracy.

- Marketing emerges as a vital function. Margin and profit are on a par with sales volume and revenues. New products, markets, and channels evolve.

- The company invests heavily in systems development. Manual and/or semiautomated order processing, fulfillment, and billing no longer works. Systems are seen as having great potential for cost reduction.

- Capital requirements keep growing. Though expenditures for customer acquisition and infrastructure improvements will be beneficial, it takes money.

- The reporting of financial results and operational metrics is more formal and encompassing. The company is increasingly managed "by the numbers."

- Middle management has evolved to the point where it is capable of running most of the company's tactical operations. The critical importance of middle management competence is fully realized.

- Strategic thinking and planning is becoming a full-time job for the senior management team. The prospects of potential mergers/acquisitions and an IPO loom in the future.

- Control of the company has become diluted by additional rounds of financing. The original founders and investors may no longer dominate the board.

- Competency deficiencies have surfaced at all levels of the business; some founders are replaced on the senior management team.

Maturity

- A reconstituted senior management team is in place with a mix of founders and new additions. The team will remain stable assuming the ongoing success of the company.

- The business is well funded; the team is not overly concerned with short to medium-term financing of the company.

- Middle management is fully engaged in running the day-to-day operations of the company.

- Mergers, acquisitions (to continue growth), and/or the prospect of an IPO (to fund growth) are the dominant areas of focus for senior management.

- Core systems are in place; systems enhancement for improved efficiencies and advantages in the marketplace are constantly under review.

- Business processes are in place. The inevitable bureaucracy that accompanies size creeps into the company. Cost management becomes a constant struggle.

- Marketing is one of if not the most dominant function(s) in the enterprise. New products, channels, and markets are deployed quickly. Pricing strategies have become an art.

Use these stages as a guide. There are no hard-and-fast rules, but they are a road map and provide a forecast of what's to come.

HOW DO YOU KNOW IF YOU'RE GROWING TOO FAST?

The last section began with a list of indicators showing whether growth is of the "plain old" variety or is sustainable and profitable. However, the manifestations of unbridled growth go far beyond those few. Companies must be constantly vigilant of a growth pace that exceeds the company's ability to deal with it.

Sales Volume and Revenue: A Brief Primer

Key early stage growth metrics are typically sales volume and revenue. These will always be vital to a company, but they are the dominant early indicators. The "top line" succinctly captures the company's advancement and is more easily influenced than other "lines" below.

Increased sales volume equals increased revenues. Increased revenues in early stage companies typically equal increased profit. Increased profits equal more capital to reinvest in the company. Life is good.

A major mistake is the exclusive use and interpretation of the sales/revenue scorecard. Additional indicators grow in importance as the company becomes more sophisticated, and a singular focus on sales and revenues leads to major problems.

Sales and Revenues Are Increasing at 15 percent a Month

Consider this scenario: If January sales were $100,000, you will be billing over $465,000 in December. It will be almost $2.5 million per month at the end of the next year. That's 2500 percent growth in twenty-four months! Just think what the company will be like with revenues of $2.5 million a month.

The euphoria of such anticipated growth (or a half, a third, or even a quarter of it) is intoxicating. Just imagine revenue flowing in to the company at rates three, six, twelve, or twenty-four times what it is today.

Too often, management comes to the conclusion if they can only make that kind of revenue growth a reality, the company is well on its way to phenomenal success. With that assumption, a preponderance of management's energy, time, and focus is spent on making that sales growth happen.

Many executives, particularly entrepreneurs, share a common perspective:

> Sales and revenues are a positive topic and fun to talk about and get involved with; costs and expenses are a negative topic and are not fun to talk about and get involved with.

This inclination coupled with the thrill of rapid increases in revenue can distract senior management from paying proper attention to the back office and infrastructure requirements. Management tends to rationalize away the resource requirements inherent in supporting the "sexy" sales forecasts.

RATIONALIZATION IS A TERRIBLE THING

The following statements come from imaginary executives of a hypothetical company who anticipate a very significant upturn in sales. The topic under discussion is how the "back office" will cope.

- "Let's handle it with overtime as long as we can."
- "We can increase the waiting time for customers calling the support center; after all, we probably are delivering a higher level of service than our competitors anyway."
- "Our time intervals for shipping/fulfillment can slip a little bit; most customers won't notice."
- "If we remove one of our quality assurance steps there probably won't be an appreciable increase in complaints or returns."
- "Collections are good. Taking a small hit there won't matter much."
- "Let's delay the systems upgrade until we get past this sales spike. We won't be able to take the reps off the phone for training."
- "I think we should bring in some temporary employees to get us over the hump."
- "We've only got room for a few more people in our ops center, but with some shift changes and a little crowding I think we can get by."

These statements represent the first step on a slippery slope leading to chaos and potentially fatal problems. A thin line exists between creative solutions and obstinacy manifested by the refusal to acknowledge problems head-on and deal with complicated and expensive solutions.

Sales and Infrastructure: Beware of Separate and Unequal Growth

Rather than calling for infrastructure emphasis equaling that of revenue growth, the back office (production/fulfillment, customer support, MIS, process development, HR competencies, and so on) must receive *more* emphasis and receive that emphasis *immediately* upon the beginning of the sales growth *if not before*.

It takes less time to ramp up selling activities than it does to beef up the support infrastructure. This is not a recommendation that companies build new factories and overstaff customer service, hoping that "since it has been built, the customers will come." No company can afford such a luxury. However, the opposite approach of ignoring back office requirements is no less foolish.

Management must realize the time lags incumbent in building support infrastructure. Hiring takes time. Training takes time. Everything required to support the product and customer after the sale takes time.

The fulfillment, operations, and support functions must receive the resources and senior management attention required to support increased sales volume. Ideally, they will always be one step ahead. A successful service company we are familiar with insured that its customer support staff was hired, trained, and in place at least sixty days before they were actually needed to support growth in the customer base.

So, when are you growing too fast?

The answer: When you no longer have the ability to provide your customers the quality product and support they have come to expect, and/or when the company's internal expectations can no longer be met.

Warning Signs

Following is an expanded list of indicators that a company is growing beyond its ability to cope with it.

- Senior management is almost exclusively focused on increased sales/revenue.
- Employee turnover and absenteeism increase, particularly for first-level supervisors.
- Customer complaints/returns are on the increase.
- Overtime increases.

- Backlogs develop in production/fulfillment.
- Customer churn increases.
- Command and control begins to fall apart in the back office; managers and supervisors simply can't cope with the internal and external pressures.
- Product/service quality deteriorates.
- Customer billing adjustments increase.
- Bad debt write-offs increase.
- The sales organization howls that sales are deteriorating due to support problems.
- Bills go out late; Accounts Receivables (A/R) aging increases.

Finally, the cycle is complete:
The infrastructure and back office problems caused by too much growth all of a sudden disappear, but for the wrong reason. Things have gotten so bad that sales dramatically decrease and the growth is over; not the preferable way to solve the problem.

BUILDING AN AIRPLANE WHILE YOU'RE FLYING IT: THE VIRTUES OF SPEED AND FLEXIBILITY

"Speed and urgency" were identified above as overarching requirements of management in a high-growth environment. This chapter elaborates on that truism. The title of this section vividly captures the challenges and seeming impossibility of the task of managing a high-growth company. However, it can be done, and, to insure sustained growth, it must be done.

Is Everyone Equipped to Deal with This Environment?

The short answer, no! While not attempting to dive into the complexities of personalities and human behavior (which we are woefully ill equipped to do), it is useful to generally address a human characteristic that is relevant to a high-growth business: tolerance for uncertainty.

It is always risky to generalize, but it's fairly safe to assume that growth companies have more volatile and dynamic environments than established large corporations. Change exists everywhere, but it's a relative concept. Some aspects of a large company certainly do change, but the basic organizational structure and the way a large company conducts business is stable, despite what those in it may think. Everything is in play in a high-growth firm.

The relative stability of established companies attracts employees who are comfortable with the constancy it offers. They excel with this solid foundation under them, and both they and their employer benefit from their contributions. However, the environment in high-growth companies is far from stable; dynamic and fluid descriptors don't do it justice.

The leadership of high-growth companies must not only tolerate the unstable environment they're in, but thrive in it. As pilots of the airplane that is being constructed while in flight, senior management must take daily surprises in stride. Dramatic and almost instant changes in the marketplace, unpredictable moves by competitors, and unanticipated requirements for capital can't fluster them. More important, the company cannot afford for the employee body to sense confusion and panic in their leadership.

Beware of Recalcitrant Crew Members

Being at ease with change is not a trait that is desired only in management. Employees have to deal with it, too. And resistance to change and discomfort with uncertainty at lower levels in the firm can have a paralyzing effect. This resistance may be subtle and hard to detect, but senior management must be constantly vigilant.

Clearly understanding that change is constant will redefine the expectations of those individuals who are salvageable. That sounds unduly harsh, but, as stated above, some people simply cannot cope with the stress of uncertainty. And, simply telling the employees that "the only constant is change" in a meeting will not suffice.

Communications and education are the primary tools to minimize malcontent caused by the vibrant environment. But, employees who are frustrated and stressed out by their ever-changing workplace may exhibit their dissatisfaction in ways harmful to the company. Many may simply "tune out." However, others may attempt to spread their discontent.

Just another issue for senior management to be aware of.

On Top of Everything Else, Someone Is Shooting at the Airplane

While the management team is busily building the plane while it's in flight, an assortment of antiaircraft batteries are taking aim and firing away.

- Customers fire away with new demands and expectations.
- Lawmakers and regulators are amply armed with rounds and rounds of rule changes and red tape.
- Competitors do what you would expect them to do, try to blast you out of the sky constantly.
- Technology changes have some of the most effective armaments; they seem to invent a new missile every day.
- And, the financial community seems to enjoy throwing a grenade into the cockpit every now and then.

The Countermeasures: Speed and Agility

It is fitting to conclude this chapter with a discussion of the obvious: the intense need for high-growth companies to remain agile and move very quickly.

Companies must master the art of making very good decisions and making them very quickly. They must constantly reassess past decisions and incorporate what they learn in the decisions they will be making. This decision-making process must have enough formality to insure quality yet be flexible enough to turn on a dime when the variables change. Senior management must never allow bureaucracy to slow down its decision-making and strategy implementation.

Management must be the quickest of the quick thinkers and have keen and intense perception. Perceiving trends before anyone else in the industry spots them, then running the ideas through the meat-grinder of analysis and consensus-building will keep the plane flying. Accurately reading the crystal ball by not missing any clues is the key.

Here are the three easy steps to building a company that will enjoy the benefits of sustainable growth:

Identify the issues, quickly.
Make good decisions, quickly.
Take action, quickly.

Nothing to it. Just clearly understand the world in which your company exists, and master the Six Core Competencies.

Chapter 2

SUSTAINING GROWTH THROUGH ENHANCED CUSTOMER LOYALTY

ENHANCING CUSTOMER LOYALTY: IS IT REALLY THAT BIG A DEAL?

The answer is: yes, and it always will be unless your company happens to be a monopoly!

As a growth company, it's only a big deal if you have the fortunate situation of having an unlimited market, no significant competitors, and an incredible sales machine that allows you to "sell through" customer churn. And, even if any of those scenarios apply to your company, how much growth and profit opportunity goes unrealized if you're losing profitable customers that you really want to keep?

Chapter 2 looks at the first core discipline: enhancing customer loyalty. The remainder of the book not only poses questions, but provides answers, the ways and means, to master the disciplines. Here we will look at the reasons (some not as obvious as you may think) for keeping customers, how to gain an understanding of how your customers define "value" and what's really important to them, the importance of every single interaction the customer has with your company, and how to insure that false expectations are not inadvertently created for your customers.

The Relevance of Customer Loyalty To Young Growth Companies

Customer loyalty is disproportionately more critical to smaller growth firms than to larger companies simply because smaller companies are likely in an early growth mode and have not acquired a large enough customer base to withstand a high percentage of customer defections. And, corporate emphasis is almost always focused on acquiring new customers. Sadly, keeping existing customers often becomes a priority only after attrition of the existing customer base becomes a significant problem. At that point, however, efforts to retrofit the organization to a "loyalty" orientation are difficult, expensive, and time-consuming. Building that culture from the beginning is certainly preferable, and not nearly as painful.

The Numbers

We will bombard you with statistics in this chapter. The reason: It is our intent to "get your attention" early and often regarding customer loyalty. Customer churn is a silent killer, and informing you of just how deadly is a task we take very seriously. You may have seen these statistics before, but please refresh your memory and assess how well your company is doing.

- In her book *Customer Loyalty*, Jill Griffin concludes that companies can **boost profits 25 to 85 percent** by increasing customer retention by as little as 5 percent.[1]
- In *Managing Customer Value*, Bradley Gale's research uncovered the following differences in financial indices between inferior service providers and superior service providers:[2]

Table 2.1 The Numbers

	Inferior Service Providers	Superior Service Providers
ROI	11%	31%
Market Value To Investment Multiple	1.5	2.7
Cash Flow To Sales	–2.0%	2.3%

- It costs five times as much on average to attract a new customer as to keep one you already have.
- A leading U.S. manufacturer found that a customer giving it a rating of "very satisfied" is six times more likely to repurchase than those

rating it "somewhat satisfied." (Those that leave aren't going to fall into either category.)

Do we have your attention?

Customer Retention: It Doesn't Matter until It Matters

We are continually surprised by how little many companies know about their existing customers. This again is particularly pronounced in early growth companies, where so much emphasis is placed on acquiring new customers.

Typically, companies learn all they possibly can about prospective customers. Great effort, resources, and attention are dedicated to identifying, segmenting, and qualifying prospective customers. Revenue per new customer is calculated. Sales/marketing expenses are scrutinized, yielding acquisition costs per customer. Data is gathered and analysis is conducted to define benefits. Then, elaborate sales and marketing plans are developed and implemented with much fanfare.

All these activities are necessary and completely worthwhile. The issue here is not to question the validity of developing and implementing effective customer acquisition strategies, but to simply pose one question: Relative to customer acquisition, how much time and effort is spent on customer retention?

As we pointed out earlier, many companies, in the euphoric times of rapid growth, are so focused on acquisition that retention is rarely if ever a front-burner issue until something throws a wrench into the sales machine. Then, as sales volume declines everyone wants to know what's wrong. And, to take our scenario a little further, during the analysis of why the numbers aren't as good as they used to be, someone stumbles upon the fact that the problem is not just a decline in sales; retention is discovered as an issue. And, it probably has been one for quite a while, but nobody knew or much cared.

Rapid sales growth has many obvious benefits. However, large month-over-month sales increases can hide many sins, and one of them may be a customer retention problem. When sales flatten out and everyone starts asking questions, often the retention problem is discovered. Thus, two problems now exist:

• Sales are down ("Yeah, we know that.")
• Customers are leaving ("Oh my God, we didn't know that.")

And there are so many means of understanding why your current customers may be leaving. There are many ways to determine their expectations and why or how you're not meeting them:

- Complaint solicitation
- Trailer or post-transaction surveys
- Mystery shopping
- Customer panels and advisory boards
- Website questionnaires
- Periodic/formal mail, telephone, and/or face-to-face surveys
- Surveys of frontline, customer-contact employees

But the key is feedback that is: ongoing, candid, gathered from multiple sources, analyzed for trends, and followed up on.

As management drills deeper into the problems, it may discover another phenomenon: When sales were really good, the company was able to "sell through" customer churn. That is, sales volume was high enough to replace customers who were leaving and add new ones at such a rate that the growth curve was maintained.

Then, plain old arithmetic begins to take charge. Dynamics are at work that can lead to a "train wreck."

- As the company expands, sales volume must increase dramatically in terms of absolute numbers in order to produce the same month-over-month percentage increases. Few companies find it possible to sustain very high growth percentages over time.
- As the customer base grows, so does the absolute number of lost customers. Even if the retention rate remains constant, the number of lost customers increases simply due to the larger size of the customer base.
- And, if the company is paying little attention to customer loyalty, the percentage of customer defections begins to inch upward also.

Thus, the "train wreck":

- Sales volume simply can't keep up the earlier pace.
- Therefore, customer churn can no longer be "sold through."
- The customer base has become much larger.
- Therefore customer defections are larger.
- And, probably larger still because customer churn rates are increasing.

The moral of the story is simple. Executives who choose to put customer loyalty initiatives into place only after sales volume fails to handle the problem may have waited too long. At a minimum, months will be required to stop the bleeding and bring equilibrium back to the getting/losing customers equation. And, equilibrium must be reached before growth can begin again.

When Customers "Walk," What Are They Walking Away With?

The somewhat ominous predictions above may seem melodramatic and overstated. However, we recommend that you "run the numbers" for your company using Joan Cannie's model in *Turning Lost Customers into Gold*.[3]

Average annual revenue per customer: $_____
TIMES, Average return on sales: X_____%
      = $_____
TIMES, Average customer longevity   X_____ years
      = $_____
PLUS, if you know it:

- Value of average customer increases in year-over-year revenue (customer growth, add-on sales, etc.).
- Value of existing customer referrals of new business.

Your Company's Service Is Being Compared To Everyone Else's

High-growth companies, particularly while experiencing an early growth surge, just can't get a break. Don't customers realize that your company just doesn't have the resources, expertise, and wherewithal yet to provide customer service like the big guys do? Don't they know that as soon as things stabilize a bit, when there's a little more capital available and all the processes are in place, your company will really crank up its emphasis on service?

Well, no! They could care less!

Studies have found that customers evaluate a company's service not only against direct competitors in the industry, but against *every* company that services them. Your company may be in the retail industry, and it would be natural for it to be compared against a service leader like Nordstrom. But suppose your company wholesales meat?

If you offer delivery services, it seems logical that you would be compared to FedEx. But if you are a telephone company, is it fair to be evaluated against a world-class delivery service leader?

Whether you like it or not or think it's fair, your customers are constantly comparing your service with all other service they receive, no matter the provider. Though your waking (and some supposed sleeping) hours are rightfully filled with concerns about your dominant competitor's new products and pricing strategies, your existing customers, the heartbeat of your cash flow, are constantly comparing your service with what they experienced at Disney World last summer; with the efficiency of the FedEx guy who comes by the office every afternoon; with the product knowledge exhibited by the L.L.Bean rep when they were exchanging a blouse; and, believe it or not, with the elegant professionalism of the concierge at the Ritz Carlton when asked for simple directions to a restaurant.

Service competition is tough...real tough.

LOYAL CUSTOMERS DEMAND VALUE: WHAT IS VALUE?

All too often, "value" has a connotation related specifically to product and price, but in reality value is simply the relationship that customers perceive between what they "get" and what they have to "pay." But the "get" is made up of much more than the product, and the "pay" is similarly much more than just the price paid.

Growth companies are particularly susceptible to adopting the limited, product/price interpretation of value. Certainly an innovative product offered at an attractive price relative to those of its competitors does deliver value to customers, and as long as the product retains some elements of uniqueness and/or is sold at a price lower than the competition, the company's value proposition in the marketplace is valid and effective. And, typically, product innovation and/or price characterizes what many early stage high-growth companies offer the market. But what happens when the product's uniqueness and price advantages are neutralized or surpassed by the competition? There aren't many options. Either develop new innovative products or cut prices...or create value via service quality.

The Obvious "Gets" and "Pays"

Just what do customers get when they buy the product? Well, they received a physical object or were delivered a service (not to be confused with customer service in the broader context). The product has certain physical characteristics and features. And, the customer receives benefits resulting from those physical characteristics and features. The trousers arrive. The phone line is installed. The airplane lands at the appointed time. The drill press is delivered. The tires are mounted. The patient is admitted to the hospital.

In short, the customer "gets" the benefits of the literal product received or service delivered.

The customers/passengers/patients in the above examples also have an obvious "pay." They paid a price or fee for what they received. They rationally weighed the benefits to be received with the money they would part with and determined the transaction would be of net benefit to them.

Other "Gets" and "Pays" Will the customers/passengers/patients "pay" something else if the following happens?

- The trousers don't fit.
- The phone line has a hum in it.
- The plane arrives late.
- The drill press has a mechanical defect.
- The tires are misaligned.
- The hospital botches the patient's insurance paperwork.

You bet they will, and they know it. You can be assured they perceive the cost to have gone up tangibly or intangibly. What is hassle worth in the minds of customers? Even if they spend no more cash, they have to "pay" more.

Well, "stuff happens" you may say. Yes it does, and we'll discuss that in more detail later when we address the concept of recovery, but the point here is: Screw-ups aren't free for your company. You may think they are, but your customers will conclude that they are paying more. The question is, how much more will they "pay" before they decide your "price" is too high and move on?

Now, let's change the scenarios:

- The trousers arrive; they fit, and enclosed with them is a coupon for a discount for further purchases and a real "thank you" note for your business.
- The phone line works fine; someone calls to advise you that the installation has been completed and to insure that the line is functioning satisfactorily.
- The plane arrives on time; there's a gate agent awaiting you who actually has a real interest in getting you to your connecting flight on time and does what she can to help you.
- The drill press works fine; you received absolutely clear installation and operating instructions, with a toll-free number where the service representatives actually have enough product knowledge to help you when you need it.

- The tires are balanced and aligned properly; the customer receives a "thank you for your business" letter within a few days along with a customer-friendly checklist on tire care...inflation, balancing, road hazards, and so on.
- The hospital handles all the admittance paperwork properly; they then take the time to brief the patient's loved ones about those little things that will be so helpful...where to park, locations of in-hospital and outside food service locations, and the like. And, all this information is also presented in a professional, easy-to-understand packet.

Do these customers/passengers/patients perceive they "got" more for their money? More than likely, yes. They didn't go through some elaborate mental quantification process, but it's certain they believe they're getting more for their money.

So...with the first case of examples, the customers "pay" more by means of the hassles the companies put them through. In the second, the customers "get" more because not only are they not hassled, they "get" something they didn't pay for.

It's every company's choice: Make customers "pay" more or make sure they "get" more. Companies may not know if they are making their customer pay more or giving them more...but the customers figure it out soon enough.

Service Quality: The Often Ignored Value Creator

With the above anecdotal foundation laid, we present what we call the "Value Triangle."

Figure 2.1 The Value Triangle

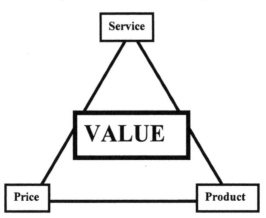

Both the concept and its representation are quite simple. The customer's ultimate determination of value will be driven by all three elements, not just the bottom two. The traditional components, product and price, form the foundation for value creation, but the great "wild card" so many companies fail to take advantage of, particularly those in the early rapid-growth stage, is service quality.

Let's look at the three elements that form customers' perceived value, with an eye toward which of the three are more easily controlled by management.

- Product: New products or product alterations can be undertaken. However, in most cases such an effort is difficult, time-consuming, and costly. A new breakthrough product can be terribly expensive.
- Price: Easily done but with significant ramifications. Lowering prices certainly positively alters customers' get/pay equation, but at what price to the company? Where does this spiral end?
- Service Quality: Just how hard is it to be nice to customers?

Okay, so we oversimplified this a little, but the point stands. In most cases, companies can impact service quality more cost-effectively, more rapidly, and with less drain on the bottom line than with new product introductions or price reductions. However, there is a caveat. Service quality often revolves around culture as much as process. Therefore, established companies that have distinctly poor service quality cultures will have a difficult time adjusting.

But, early-stage growth companies have an easier time of it. In fact, many have significant strategic opportunities to utilize service quality as a differentiator and may not know it. Their culture is in a formative stage; the blackboard is clean. There are likely fewer negative things that need "fixing." There are hundreds of employees, not tens of thousands.

We implore these early-stage high-growth companies in particular to take a serious look at the potential of using service quality as a strategic differentiator. Create value at a fraction of the cost of pursuing the other alternatives available. Rate your company using the accompanying self-assessment table, and "strive for the fives."

You Must Know What's Important to Your Customers

Very few companies overtly ignore the desires of their customers. Likewise, few don't acknowledge the importance of providing quality service in the pursuit of enhanced customer loyalty. However, many

Table 2.2 "Pay"/"Get" Assessment

Customer "Pay" Orientation	1 2 3 4 5	Customer "Get" Orientation
Customer owns an object		Customer owns a memory
The goal of product production/ delivery is uniformity		The goal of product production/ delivery is uniqueness
The product can be put into inventory		The product is all-inclusive and perishable
The customer is an end user who is not involved in the production process		The customer is a coproducer and a partner throughout
Quality consists of comparing outputs to specifications		Quality consists of customers comparing their expectations and perceptions
If improperly produced, the product will be pulled off the line		If improperly performed, planned recovery is usually the only effective means of recourse
Positive morale of employees is important and desired		Positive morale of employees is critical and necessary

never take the concept beyond lip service, or, in those cases where proactive efforts are made, they are undertaken within the context of what the *companies* think is important to their customers rather than what their *customers* actually view as significant.

Stated another way, many organizations attempt to deliver service based on what they think the customers want or what the company wants to/is capable of delivering. So, senior management executives must ask themselves several fundamental questions if/ when they decide whether or not they want to actually deliver high-quality service:

- Do we believe service quality is actually of strategic importance to the organization?
- Are we prepared to take more than cursory steps to deliver service quality?
- Do we actually believe that service quality standards should be determined by the customers' expectations?
- Once we determine the customers' expectations, are we committed to taking the measures necessary to really make it happen?

The Basics

Extensive research over the last few years has identified the generic dimensions with which customers form expectations, and their perceptions of how companies are living up to them.

- **Reliability:** the ability to perform versus the promises made; keeping the promise.
- **Responsiveness:** willingness to help customers; readiness to serve.
- **Assurance:** knowledge and courtesy of employees and their ability to convey trust and competence; "I made the right choice."
- **Empathy:** caring and individualized attention provided to customers; commitment to the customer.
- **Tangibles:** appearance of facilities, equipment, personnel, communications, materials, etc.; what the customer sees.

These service quality basics seem so self-evident, but, as all of us reflect on our personal encounters, they obviously aren't common sense to all organizations. Using the industries noted in the scenarios in the last section as examples, just what do these dimensions mean?

The Dimensions Are Great. Now Can We Get Started?

The generic dimensions are informative, but are they enough to begin designing and implementing a service quality/loyalty program? The answer is a resounding no, but many executives undertake the challenge knowing far less than the minimal information offered in the definitions of the dimensions. They draw from that ever-accurate source of irrefutable data, their collective intuition.

Lest we not appear too cynical, pleasing customers and keeping them is not a mind-boggling concept. We offer our criticism of intuition to help guide companies away from often unnecessary, nonproductive efforts and expenditures, not to chastise them. Though common sense permeates the provision of quality service, it has led to situations where companies have gone to great length to fix things they thought needed fixing, only to find out later that the customers couldn't have cared less.

An example comes to mind. A midsize technology company decided that 24/7 customer service was something their customers wanted and absolutely had to have. Although the company's call center was staffed for a couple of hours before and after normal business hours in all applicable time zones, intuition indicated to management

Table 2.3 Dimensions of Service Quality

	Reliability	Responsiveness	Assurance	Empathy	Tangibles
Mail Order Apparel	Proper sizing	Time to receipt	Return policy	Questions regarding care	Quality of packaging and promo material
Communications Company	Phone works	Repair time	Knowledge of service reps	Call center rep handling; changes in service	Truck, installation personnel
Airline	Depart & arrive on schedule	Prompt information	Safety record	Anticipates customer needs	Aircraft, terminal facilities
Industrial Manufacturer	Product performs	Speed of production	Product guarantee	Handling of requests for product tailoring	Quality of packaging, setup, and operating instructions
Tire Retailer/ Automotive Service	Problems fixed/ service delivered when promised	No waiting	Knowledgeable mechanics	Remembers previous problems/ purchases	Repair facility
Hospital	Diagnosis proven accurate	Willingness to listen	Reputation	Acknowledges patient as a person	Waiting room/ admissions area

that 24/7 was the way to go. At no small expense, personnel were added, schedules altered, and notifications sent out to the customers advising them of the new hours of operation. The change was implemented flawlessly. However, they received very few calls outside of the original hours of operation.

This is a classic example of a situation where good intentions coupled with a lack of hard information about the customers' desires led to a misallocation of resources. The new 24/7 hours of operation didn't much improve service quality. And, it could have actually hurt because there were other service quality areas where the resources could have been better spent, to solve problems that customers really had instead of a phantom problem the company thought it had.

Okay. How Do I Determine What's Important To My Customers?

The answer is straightforward and more or less the same as for prospective customers: market research. However, gathering preferences and expectations for existing customers offers fewer challenges than assessing prospects. So why do so few early-stage growth companies do it?

Look at the advantages of surveying existing (or even past) customers compared to conducting research about prospective customers:

- You know them; they know you.
- They see an obvious benefit in cooperating with a company they already buy from.
- You know what they buy; they know what you sell.
- They have real experiences with your company; there's no need to speculate.
- They have an incentive for you to serve them better.

The logistical advantages and relative ease of developing a data gathering protocol for existing customers should make it a "no-brainer." Can you still spend a lot? Yes, but you don't have to. We believe there are three basic ways of discovering what your customers really think. Though, as with most things, you can spend what you want to, and the more you spend the more precise read you will have on your customers. But, no matter which route you take, you'll be better off than not doing anything.

In-depth, formal research, with which you are all familiar even if in a market/prospective customer context. Typically, outside research firms are engaged to develop thoughtful, statistically accurate analyses. Endless time can be spent just on the formulation of questions, and very sophisticated data gathering and analytical tools are employed.

The "customer scorecard," in concept, usually a relatively simple survey sent to a representative sample of the customer base that asks them to identify and rank order two basic lists: 1) issues with/ expectations of the company, and 2) how well the company is performing on each. This cross-reference of the "how important" and "how well" defines areas of improvement and focus...from the customers' perspective.

Ask your employees who deal with customers every day as a replacement for direct customer input, and preferably an augmentation. Employee research yields valuable data from the hundreds or thousands of customer encounters that occur every day. Suppose the technology company we referred to earlier had asked its employees how many complaints they had received from customers who needed access to 24/7 service?

We've barely scratched the surface of a subject of critical importance, but hope we've gotten the message across. Once you have decided that quality service is important to your organization, take the time to find out what the customers think in order to insure that you're focusing the firm's time, talent, and resources on things that will truly make a difference and improve customer loyalty.

Every Contact with the Customer: A Blessing or a Disaster?

Well, like many things in life, it depends.

And it depends on all the employees who have any interactions with customers and/or are involved with any facet of the business that interacts with customers. And, it depends on how well those employees are equipped and prepared to insure that those encounters are perceived as value-adds by the customers.

Moments of Truth

Jan Carlzon of Scandinavian Airlines in his book *Moments of Truth* coined the term "moments of truth" in describing these customer encounters, and no phrase could better capture the essence of the concept.[4] The statements above are intentionally broad in scope and inclusive, and are so by intent. Whether a company produces a product or delivers a service like Scandinavian Airlines, it has dozens of encounters with customers. Each of which will be a moment when the truth is disclosed about whether or not the company, in reality, delivers what its customers want. Some are obvious, others less so.

Human encounters are perhaps the most obvious and critical. The demeanor of the salesperson, the responsiveness of the customer service representative, and the competence of the service technician all provide a company opportunities to create a "blessing" in terms of meeting/exceeding customer expectations. Conversely, opportunities exist for "disasters." We'll address human encounters in more detail in a moment.

But there are more subtle yet critical interfaces with customers that may not immediately come to mind. As you review the following list, determine how your company is managing these indirect "moments."

- Your invoice: Was it designed with the ease of customers' use paramount or the ease of the company in printing it?
- Promotional collateral/direct mail: Is it so self-centered in terms of the information the company wants to communicate that it overlooks what customers may want to know?
- Adjustments and credits: Does the reimbursement process deliver checks to customers as quickly as you want to receive checks from them?
- The website: Does it present the information and functionality that make it easy for customers to navigate and use?
- Your phone system: Does its design focus on customer friendliness or corporate efficiency goals?
- Scheduling of delivery: Does the process allow for the scheduling realities of two-income households and their need for specificity, or are half-day windows all the company offers?

Balancing Processes and Judgment

As we noted, the primary and most critical "moments" occur when your customers encounter your employees. Rarely are these encounters viewed as completely neutral by your customers; they're either positive or negative to one degree or another in their eyes. Most companies realize this and constantly strive to initiate processes and business rules to insure that customers are satisfied yet not overwhelmed with "company policies."

Large established companies have usually matured to the point that they have about all the policies their customers can stand. And, smaller but emerging companies tend to have fewer policies, sometimes intentionally, but usually because process development in the company as a whole has yet to mature.

What is best? Do you get really good people and provide the ambiguous guidance to "do the right thing"? Or do you move to the other end of the spectrum and try to write a rule for every occasion?

This decision is particularly relevant to early-stage growth firms. Remember, they have the clean blackboards. There are fewer problems from the past to solve so they have the fortunate circumstance of generally "creating" and not "correcting." With that assumption in mind, following are thoughts on dealing with the ever-present conundrum of trying to figure out how much process and how much judgment to build into the guidance you provide your customer contact personnel.

Service Quality Process Development

Companies in the entrepreneurial stage consciously or unconsciously utilize the "do the right thing" approach in preparing their employees to deal with customers. There are relatively few employees, and most of them are aware of most aspects of the company's operation. The founding management team either instilled a customer orientation or it didn't, and the employees follow suit. It's natural. Employees follow their bosses' examples, be they good or bad.

However, as we discuss in a later chapter, growth requires the development of processes and business rules across the board. And, standards for service quality are no different. At some point, whether good or bad practices have developed informally, things have to get organized and systematized.

This is a critical point for companies to learn. Service quality processes will either evolve with a company-centric or customer-centric orientation. The former will lead to problems that must be corrected later; conversely, if the company expands with a focus on serving its customers, it positions itself for sustainable growth.

The steps for customer-centric process development are simple and hold great promise if adopted at an early stage.

- Determine the customers' most important expectations (remember the last section).
- Define/refine the processes that have an impact on those expectations.
- Measure the output/results of those processes.

To reinforce the appeal we made in the last section, remember that without the first step, service quality process development defaults to the company-centric model. Rules are written and policies are developed with the company in mind, not the customers. Once the die is cast in that direction, the slope toward company-centricity becomes more slippery and steeper by the day, and the effort required to climb back up the slope at some point down the road will be greater. Many companies find it impossible to climb back up the slope, as the company-centric inertia built up over the years is impossible to overcome.

We remember flying on one of the major but now defunct airlines. Frequently while walking through an airport concourse we would hear passengers say that they would never fly that airline again: Flights were seldom on time, the flight attendants couldn't care less about any but the basic and routine passenger needs, the airline frequently lost baggage, and so on.

As passengers flocked to competitors, the airline laid off employees, which caused the unions to rally employees against the airline, and service deteriorated further. The cycle continued until the last days of the airline's existence, when the few employees who were left all of a sudden got the message and seemed to become genuinely interested in customer needs. It was too late. The slope was too slippery.

Have We Removed Judgment with All This Process Talk?

The authors have confidence in the power of a positive corporate culture, something we'll discuss in a later chapter. We also have great faith in what individual employees can accomplish in such a culture. We are all too familiar with the excesses of process development in larger, more mature companies, where company-centric service policies frustrate and infuriate customers daily.

However, as realists with the experience of working for/with high-growth companies, we know that growth without processes and standards quickly turns into chaos, at times even anarchy. How do we balance our disdain for cumbersome, customer-unfriendly processes and the need for order?

The following diagram presents an approach to deal with this dilemma. The horizontal axis represents the continuum of process development, from "none" (relies on individual employee judgment) to "hard processes" (tight, step-by-step guidance provided to the employee).

The vertical axis represents the continuum of importance to customers, from low to high; how important any given issue/expectation is to customers (there's only one way to find this out: Ask the customers!).

The plotted curve makes our point clearly: The less important an issue is as viewed by the customers, the less rigorous the processes required. However, for those issues viewed as important by customers, very tight processes should be developed and monitored. The

Figure 2.2 Customers and Process Development

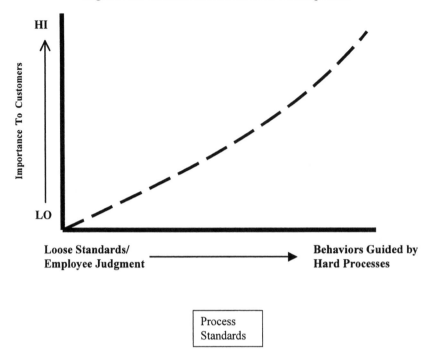

customers have told you these issues are very important to them, and you simply do not want to leave dealing with those issues to chance.

"Loose/tight" is a Tom Peters concept applied to service quality process development. Stay closely on top of those things most important to your customers.

RECOVERY: GETTING IT RIGHT THE SECOND TIME

Earlier we concluded that "stuff happens." No organization performs perfectly all the time, particularly early-stage, rapidly growing companies. Their world is chaotic, people are being hired in droves, and orders are pouring in.

Continual efforts will be made to minimize the number of breakdowns, but they will always exist. So, the real question should be: What does your company do when it screws up?; not: What can your company do to never screw up?

Complaints Are Good

Not because you screwed up, but because your customers chose to let you know that something is wrong and gave you the opportunity to do something about it! Complaining customers are really telling you:

- They care
- They think you care
- They think you have the potential to do better
- They expect to see improvement
- And, they want to continue the relationship

Dealing with complaints is far preferable to the alternative: those unhappy customers who just keep their mouths shut and leave. And, we know from research that a vast majority of those who leave do so for reasons that the company can do something about:

- 68 percent leave because of an attitude of indifference by an employee. You can do something about that.
- 3 percent move away; 14 percent leave for competitive reasons or develop other friendships that encourage them to leave; and, 14 percent are dissatisfied with the product.

It's very difficult to do anything about those.

And, customers who are unhappy with you but not dissatisfied enough to complain are going to buy from you again only 9 percent of the time. Translation: They will stay with you only until a better offer comes along; they're carrying a grudge.

But (and here's the punch line), 82 percent of complaining customers will stay with you if their complaints are resolved quickly.[5]

Handle Those Complaints Effectively!

As individuals, we've all had occasions where we've encountered both positive and negative responses to our concerns and complaints. We won't throw any more statistics at you, but most of us can testify from personal experience that when we have truly poor experiences as customers, we tell anyone who will listen; we become virtual negative propaganda machines. Hell hath no fury like a scorned customer.

Conversely, though we might not be as vocal, a positive service experience, particularly when the company recovered from a screwup, causes us to flush with satisfaction, and we tell others. Regrettably, that may be due to the fact that we don't have too many of these experiences. Think about it ... all we really want as customers when we encounter a problem is:

- For someone to listen to us and take us seriously
- For someone to understand the problem and the reason we're un-happy
- To get the problems fixed quickly
- To avoid further inconvenience
- For someone to treat us with respect
- To be assured the problem won't happen again
- To feel we are treated fairly

This is not brain surgery! Why do so many companies fail to establish effective complaint-handling and recovery processes? Though they would rarely own up to it, companies that do not proactively work at soliciting complaints and solving them have an "attitude" manifested by the following:

- They see customers as expendable; there's another one where that one came from.
- They believe their values, procedures, and processes have a life of their own ... read: company-centric.
- They think it's too difficult; after all, customers might have higher expectations after they've been abused.
- They don't think it's worth it financially. They have been living on Mars and aren't familiar with the statistics proving the value of customer loyalty.
- They've never done it before. Well, if it's always been done that way, let's not dare consider change.

Recovery/Complaint Management Assessment

Following is a list of questions we urge you to answer relative to your company. Some questions are quite tactical, some more overarching, but collectively they provide answers that will reveal your company's effectiveness in managing complaints.

However, before you answer the questions, a quick comment on "attitude." If your company thinks of complaints as nuisances, or worse, only as reasons for taking punitive measures against erring employees, there is little likelihood that this assessment will tell you much or help you. If the organization doesn't really want to know why customers are unhappy and do something about it, why go to the trouble of managing complaints effectively? If the company only wants to reprimand employees who may have violated company-centric policies, don't bother with the questions. Individual mistakes cause problems, but so do internal policies, poor processes, conflicting compensation policies, senior management focus, and company strategies. All should be open to inspection and criticism when a customer complains ... not just the service representative.

Getting complaints/inquiries to the right place and prioritizing them for action:

- What happens to complaints addressed to senior executives by name or title or to specific departments?
- Are the complaint receivers aware of where to send the complaints and the importance of immediate action?
- If a complaint call is misdirected, do their employees know where to direct the call or how to handle the call?
- What do departments other than customer service do with incoming complaints and inquiries?
- Do customer contact employees have written guidelines on how to identify and handle serious complaints?

Logging complaints/inquiries:

- Is there an access identifier or any other technique that enables the complaint to be retrieved for future action?
- Does the log contain responsibility, a target date, and action to be taken?
- Is the complaint categorized in a way to enable preventive analysis?
- If complaints are resolved immediately, is any notation made of the root cause and the complaint category?

Investigating complaints/inquiries:

- Do complaint-handling employees know where to get the information necessary to investigate a complaint?
- How long does it take to investigate a complaint?

Answering complaints/inquiries:

- Do answers usually immediately meet customer expectations or explain why the customers' expectations cannot be met?

- Do answers provide reassurance if further investigation is required to resolve the complaint or query?
- Are answers usually clear and understandable to the customer? Accurate?
- Do answers reflect the long-term benefits of repeat business?

Giving timely responses:

- Are complaints and inquiries answered within the time frame expected by customers?
- Is response time measured and reported?

Preparing reports:

- Do reports include the status of preventive recommendations?

Identifying and analyzing problems:

- Does the complaint and inquiry process also include identification of root causes and analysis of what can be done to prevent a reoccurrence?

Recommending preventive measures:

- Are recommendations presented to the appropriate managers in the organization who can correct the problem and prevent a reoccurrence?

Evaluating the function:

- Are there increasing levels of customer satisfaction and repurchase intention?

Tracking customer satisfaction:

- Is there a satisfaction tracking system to monitor satisfaction levels and repurchase intention?

Selecting, training, and developing staff:

- Are there appropriate standards for recruiting and selecting customer contact staff?
- Are new staff members given training before they begin their new jobs?
- Are there incentives or rewards and recognition programs to encourage outstanding service performance?

Getting customers to inquire and complain:

- How easy is it for customers to make an inquiry or complain?

FALSE EXPECTATIONS: A SURE PATH TO DISLOYALTY

We started this chapter by expressing the importance of customer loyalty in terms of real dollars. We emphasized later the potential of service quality differentiation, something that can make your company truly different. We talked about how vitally important it is to make the effort to understand what your customers' expectations are and build your service quality initiatives around those expectations. We provided suggestions for building service quality processes, again centered on the customers' expectations. And, in the previous section, we addressed how companies can recover when their customers' expectations are not met.

Every one of those tasks is, obviously, built around customers' expectations. Customers expect a lot in the competitive world in which we live. Their natural demands establish a high bar for companies as it is, and, getting over that bar proves challenging for all companies.

However, clearing the bar becomes next to impossible if it is raised by inflated and unrealistic customer expectations . . . concocted by the company itself!

Customers develop expectations based on any and everything the company states or infers, no matter how obtuse, fleeting, indirect, unintended, or misinterpreted. And, many customers, being natural negotiators, will leverage whatever the company has stated or inferred in efforts to receive more value from their perspective: lower prices, quicker delivery intervals, better terms and conditions, and so on.

So what's the point? Simply, any company communications that lead customers to draw incorrect conclusions and build false expectations must be avoided at all costs.

- Salespeople cannot infer that a product will do something it can't just to close the sale.
- Customer service reps can't promise a specific time for a maintenance call just because the customer is yelling at them.
- Sales and promotional material and activities can't infer that the company has capabilities that really don't exist.
- The deliveryperson can't promise a billing adjustment for late delivery if the company doesn't have a policy to issue one.

- The customer's invoice can't say "call anytime" if the call center isn't open "anytime."
- The catalog can't show a blue shirt if only red, yellow, and white shirts are available.

The list could go on and on. We're not talking about intentional fraud, misleading advertising, or outright lying in most cases. We're talking about mistakes, insinuations, and "partly cloudy" statements that, for whatever reason, create expectations the company simply cannot meet. It's tough enough to please customers as it is. Creating unattainable expectations is self-inflicted punishment at its worst.

In the end, it makes no difference if customers leave because the company could not meet either real or artificial expectations . . . they're still gone!

Chapter 3

DYNAMIC PLANNING
AND BUDGETING

HOW GOOD IS YOUR PLANNING... REALLY?

Every company has a planning process, some being more formal than others. The existing strategic/business plan is, hopefully, driving the company's decision-making and everyday execution. The management team is familiar with planning methodologies. That assumption is a given.

However, the requisite planning competencies of a high-growth company exceed those of other firms. The constantly changing environment and highly volatile nature of the company in dealing with those changes render many conventional approaches to planning obsolete. The fundamentals are the same, but the flexibility of the planning process must match the dynamics of the environment.

Our goals for this chapter are simple: 1) to provide a way for your company's planning efforts to remain relevant in the face of an ever-changing marketplace and ever-changing company; 2) to provide tools for insuring that the major components in the planning process—self-analysis, development of your value proposition, competitive analysis, targeting—remain valid; 3) to offer meaningful and realistic suggestions on how to cope with cost-cutting, something all companies face at one time or another; and, 4) to help you insure the ongoing linkage between the plans and the budget.

Eliminating Mental Scotomas

The concept of mental scotomas (permanent or temporary areas of diminished perception of the obvious) is interesting and real. One of the better examples is the apparent sudden appearance of automobiles exactly like the one you just bought once you take it out of the showroom and start driving; you see dozens just like it. They have been there all along; you just didn't "see" them until you had a reason to start "looking."

The conventional planning process is characteristically bounded by "conventional wisdom." Everyone discusses "thinking outside the box," but pushing beyond the accepted assumption set is difficult. Large companies rarely allow it at the strategic level, and many small companies are too intimidated to try it.

You cannot afford to have your thinking and planning corralled by mental scotomas. Opportunities must be identified and action taken before your competitors beat you to it. You must "see through" the filters of past experiences and conventional thinking.

The traditional planning process most companies use is sound. It will be reviewed later. But, *how* the company uses the process should be the planning differentiator.

Scotoma-Removing Questions

- Are the mission and vision of the company reactive? Or, do they indicate that the company really can do something new and different? Are they shaped by "what was" rather than "what could be"?
- Does the planning conclude that the current conditions of the industry are boundaries and constraints or something that can be redefined?
- Are you benchmarking against the "best"? Why not assume that you can be the best?
- Do you force the round peg of potential capabilities into the square hole of available resources? Or, do you view the future from the perspective of what "could" be done with additional resources?
- Are product/market expansion analyses conducted from the perspective of what has been done rather than what could be done?
- Do you plan to match your competitors? Why not innovate and completely pass them by?
- Why not create a culture that you really want in the company? Why just sit around and read the books about General Electric (GE)?
- Are breathtaking innovations in service quality possible, or do you want to just do what everyone else is doing?

As pragmatists all too aware of the realities of running a company, many executives do not allow themselves to occasionally dream. Will a "dream session" immediately identify the "Midas touch" that leads to dazzling success? Not likely. Can you expect all the ideas from brainstorming to lead major and dramatic improvements of the company's fortunes? Probably not.

However, if senior management allows an atmosphere of creativity to surround its planning process, not only will the company foster the innovation required for high growth, every so often a "gem" of brilliance will surface that just might become the elusive "Midas touch."

A Quick Assessment of the Current Plan

How do you assess your existing plans? Below are fundamental questions to ask yourself. There is no scoring for this "quiz," but if you answer "no" too many times, your plans probably need a rework.

- Do you have a formal plan?
- Has it been more than six months since the plan was formally reassessed?
- Has the plan changed significantly from the original created during the entrepreneurial stage?
- Have marketplace changes during the last twelve months been incorporated into the plan?
- Does the plan reflect changes inside the company in the last twelve months; specifically, does it incorporate changes in the company's competencies?
- Does the plan incorporate detailed knowledge of your competitors?
- Does the plan formally address the human resource requirements (quantitative and qualitative) and how they will be addressed?
- Does the plan reflect substantive legislative and/or regulatory changes that may have occurred?
- Rather than solely a compilation of the collective knowledge and wisdom of the employees, did the plan utilize external sources?
- Was the plan a collective effort of the team?
- Does a data collection mechanism exist to insure that relevant information needed for the next update of the plan is captured and organized?

Can all the executives and key managers, off the top of their heads, clearly articulate:

- The company's significant short/long-term growth goals and, generally, how they are to be achieved?
- The company's major strengths and weaknesses?
- The strategic competitors' major strengths and weaknesses?
- The company's value proposition?
- The company's strategic niche?

Internal Strengths/Weaknesses Analysis:
The Building Block of Planning

This section addresses one of the most critical elements of the planning process: the honest, thorough, and objective assessment of the company. The following chapters address three other vital, externally focused elements: your value proposition, your niche, and your competitors.

The internal S/W analysis is included in this chapter because it is the foundation upon which the plan is built. Erroneous or inaccurate assumptions flowing from poorly executed assessments lead to faulty strategies, misguided product development, and a host of other problems very difficult to correct once the course is set and the ship sails. Hundreds of Strengths/Weaknesses/Opportunities/Threats (SWOT) checklists exist, but the objective here is to try to capture those that apply to every industry.

Despite the best of intentions of management to produce credible plans, there never is enough time to devote to the process. A summary of those issues particularly relevant to the internal assessment of high-growth companies is included to assist management in determining emphasis and priorities. Clear and specific answers to the following questions provide senior management with an accurate barometer of where the company stands today.

A Brief Look Back

- What has made the company successful up to now?
- What have been the company's most significant accomplishments?
- What has it been like to work for the company?
- What did the company do that didn't work?
- What did you do about it?

The Current Look

- What are the three greatest strengths of the company; and its three greatest weaknesses?
- What are its five strongest competencies; and the five weakest?
- How well is the company performing financially? How much cash does it have?
- What are the strongest departments/functions; the weakest?
- Who are the strongest team members; the weakest?
- Can team members meet the challenges of new/expanded responsibilities?
- How scalable are the operations of the company?
- Which activities in the business have strong processes in place; which don't?

- And, what processes are automated; which aren't?
- What are the company's capabilities for finding, hiring, training, and developing employees?
- By department, how strong is the focus on the customers, be they internal or external?

A Look at the Competitors

Ideally, you would know as much about your competitors as you know about yourself. That is obviously impossible, but competitive analyses should be defined as comprising a great deal more than price comparisons between your products and theirs.

We will discuss competitive analysis in terms of "big and little fish" below, but here are a few competitive data gathering tips.

Competitors continually expose their strengths and weaknesses, and sometimes in the most unlikely places. A growth company should develop and keep current a dossier on its competitors and take advantage of the information that's either readily available or accessible with a little effort.

Following is a very brief and illustrative list of desired information, information sources, and suggestions to make the information more useful.

What Do You Need to Know?

The Basics Regrettably, many companies believe this is all they need to know about their competitors. That may be because such information is usually very easy to obtain from web sites or your own sales force.

- Product portfolio
- Pricing
- New product introduction
- Special deals or discounts
- Promotional messages/themes

The Company If your competitors are publicly traded, many sources of information exist. But, many of your competitors are not public, and here the quest for information becomes more of a challenge. Understanding the general characteristics of your opponent can prove fruitful. Their websites are jammed with information!

- The general sophistication of their website and who hosts it provide insight into their systems capabilities; whether they outsource or not.
- Do the specific capabilities of their website include online order entry and bill viewing/payment? The presence or absence of certain features provides insight into their overall systems abilities.
- Company management: Who are they, what are their experiences, where did they come from, how long have they been there?
- Press releases indicate the value they place on public relations as well as their "hot button" issues.
- Partners: Who are their suppliers? Who do they have strategic relationships with?

Street Smarts The company's sales force is perhaps its greatest potential source of competitive information. We use the word potential because few companies effectively tap this resource. Salespeople know a great deal more than they are usually given credit for. If the company values their input, lets them know it, and makes it easy for the sales force to provide this information (they simply aren't going to fill out a report once week), real-time insight of the competitors can be gained.

What Do You Do with the Information? The importance of competitive information warrants serious consideration of dedicating resources to acquire and analyze it. Your strategic planning protocol provides a format for organizing and assessing the data.

No matter what the process, effective planning requires the company to "bounce" itself against the competitors to uncover both your and their vulnerabilities. You should understand your own company; that's the fairly easy part. But, for the planning loop, the company must have well-organized competitive data readily at hand for analysis.

Remember the guiding principles of good planning:

- Allow some dreaming
- Know thyself
- Know thy enemies

DYNAMIC PLANNING

As intimated in the previous chapters, the planning effort and its output must deal with dynamics that many slow/no-growth companies don't face. All the pieces are constantly in motion, and companies must develop processes that effectively accommodate the fluid environment in which planning occurs.

Periodic Reassessment: "Quarterly Timeouts"

Traditionally, formal planning is an annual affair. Typically, planning retreats or other scheduled activities are initiated at some point prior to the budgeting process. Whether considerable preparation is conducted (the suggested regimen) or the sessions are postured as brainstorming exercises, the effort produces an assessment of where the company currently stands and a broad, future-looking course of action...certainly for a year, maybe for multiple years.

There is great value in this exercise. The day-to-day rigors of running the business seldom allow quiet time to assess the future. However, for growth companies the marketplace as well as the company itself will have changed by the time the plan is printed and distributed. This leads to management frustration, whether conscious or unconscious. The whole planning exercise and the effort required seem only marginally productive and, regrettably, result in a lack of confidence in the plan. And, without good planning, the company returns to a tactical, reactive mode rationalized by its inability to integrate constant change into the process.

The solution is a planning process that accommodates change, does not frustrate management, and has the built-in flexibility to produce meaningful outputs. That process is to schedule streamlined *quarterly* planning reassessments.

A major challenge for "streamlined" planning is the requirement to do it expeditiously while simultaneously producing meaningful results. Let us acknowledge again our awareness of management's overwhelming day-to-day responsibilities and time constraints. Any quarterly process not accomplished in a day or less simply will not be embraced and, more important, will be viewed as a waste of time. If brevity is not achieved, the effort will certainly turn out to be just that...a waste of time.

The Analysis Grid

The Analysis Grid (Table 3.1) is a summary of internal and external assessments made in the annual strategic planning session. It is the tool used in conducting quarterly plan reviews and making strategic adjustments. The grid simply summarizes internal and external factors and forms the basis for easy ongoing adjustments. Here's our recommendation on how to use the grid most effectively.

- At the conclusion of the annual planning session or review of the existing plan, rate the company on the scale of 1 to 5 for each of the environmental and competency/capabilities on the grid. That's no more than two pages.
- Document the major assumptions used in establishing the ratings; limit to no more than five pages.
- On a quarterly basis, the senior management team should schedule a "timeout" session lasting no more than a day. The executives should review the seven-page document prior to the session.

The agenda for the timeout is straightforward:

- Review the prior ratings and assumptions.
- Identify significant changes in the environment or company that would lead to a rating change.
- Change the rating and document the assumptions.
- Review the strategies from the original analysis and determine if adjustments should be made.
- Make any necessary adjustments and communicate them to the organization.

The grid and agenda are applicable to any business in any industry. You may modify or augment the items identified. However, the value of the approach lies in its simplicity and focus on the major issues impacting the company's plans and strategies. Hundreds of additional, valid issues could be addressed and discussed, but a laserlike focus on those that really matter produces the necessary concentrated thinking and effort.

The recommended "quarterly timeouts" produce several tangible and meaningful benefits:

- They provide for orderly analysis and change.
- They maintain the plan's timeliness and meaningfulness.
- They reinforce the concept of active rather than static planning.
- They force senior management into a strategic thinking mode on a scheduled basis.
- They lessen the "reality versus the plan" frustrations of management.

Table 3.1 Analysis Grid

	Low Rating Characteristics	1	2	3	4	5	High Rating Characteristics
The Environment							
State of the Economy	No growth; recession						High growth; little inflation
State of the Industry	No growth, declining						High growth
Government/Regulatory	Highly regulated; potentially significant impact on business plan						Little, no regulation; no/little impact on business plan
General Competitive Environment	Very competitive; large, well-financed competitors						Low/moderately competitive; many small/medium competitors
Marketplace	Unstable; high fluctuations in demand and prices						Stable; steady demand and prices
Company Capabilities/ Competencies							
Planning	Informal, ad hoc, tactical, and reactive						Formal, flexible, continual
Senior Management/ Leadership	Inexperienced; little industry knowledge; major gaps in functional knowledge						Experienced, smooth-running team; functional leadership in place and mature
Middle Management	Not in place; immature and/or ineffective						Capable of running the day-to-day business
Capital/Funding	Minimal capital; low potential of acquiring more						Funded business plan
Sales	Single and/or immature channel(s); unsophisticated if any command/control and development activities						Multiple, mature, integrated channels; strong channel management

Table 3.1 (*Continued*)

	Low Rating Characteristics	1	2	3	4	5	High Rating Characteristics
Marketing (general)	Nonexistent or immature; subservient to Sales						Formalized; competent oversight and guidance of channels, pricing, products
Product Development	No process; ad hoc or reactive; slow to market						Highly organized; cross-functional teams; quick to market
Technological Infrastructure	Manual processes; rudimentary automation; systems that don't interface with each other						Highly automated and integrated systems across all business functions
Production/Fulfillment	Low productivity/quality; high customer complaints and churn						High productivity/quality; high customer loyalty
Processes/Business Controls	Few if any; sporadic, uncoordinated among the business functions						Corporate-wide process orientation; all mission-critical processes in place; others in progress
HR Capabilities (employee acquisition, retention, development)	No centralized HR function; no hiring, evaluation, promotion standards; no compensation policies						Centralized HR; hiring, training, development processes in place; performance management present
Regulatory/Public Policy	Ineffective monitoring of rules/regulations; mandatory reports late, fines incurred						Monitoring and compliance processes in place; involvement in industry associations; active policy advocacy (if appropriate)
Morale	High employee turnover; numerous performance and behavior problems						Low turnover; highly motivated employees, which leads to excellent customer service performance

We have observed that this approach causes executives, often for the first time, to:

- begin openly and candidly sharing their strategic thoughts with their peers
- have an energized dialogue around critical business issues *before* the "planning session" actually gets under way
- develop an enhanced sense of esprit de corps because they realize their thoughts are shared by other members of the executive team

YOUR VALUE PROPOSITION

This section and the next two address three critical components of the planning process, your value proposition, your niche, and your competitors. Clearly determining what/who they are and how they impact the business is absolutely mandatory. They are determined by assessing the environment and the company's capabilities. Complete clarity of definition is a prerequisite for sustained growth.

What Is a Value Proposition?

The term entered the business lexicon about ten years ago and has become a popular buzzword. It is used and misused in a variety of ways, but its original purpose was to succinctly summarize a company's uniqueness and the benefits that uniqueness brings to the major constituencies of the company—the customers, the shareholders, and the employees. In relatively few words, it should capture the company's mission/vision and be employed to bring value to the customers, wealth to the shareholders, and a sense of fulfillment to the employees.

In short, the company's value proposition is its ultimate statement of focus and communicates the reasons for its existence.

Why Is It So Important?

The words consistency and focus appear often throughout this book. An overriding theme is that growth companies exist in a very dynamic, ever-changing world. Both the environment and the company are in a constant state of flux. The ever-present distractions, frantic pace, and challenges of growth can be dealt with only by having a solid foundation in place. That foundation (the value proposition) must possess several non-negotiable characteristics:

- It states the company's "deliverables" to its constituencies
- There is no ambiguity of intent and ultimate outcome
- It is succinct, direct, and easily understood
- It can be articulated by all with ease and confidence

Components of the Value Proposition

Value propositions vary greatly from company to company, but the universal commonality is that it expresses a clear uniqueness for the company. If a company cannot create and express uniqueness in its value proposition, if it simply restates what fifteen other competitors are trying to do, the company's ability to sustain growth is in doubt. Why? If your company isn't capable of doing something identifiably different from the competitors, no reason exists for the customers to buy your product, for investors to provide capital or, ultimately, for your employees to come to work.

Elements that can create uniqueness:

- The product itself; something no one else has; the Hummer
- Price; no one else offers similar value at a lower price; AirTran Airlines
- Customer loyalty; no one else takes better care of the customers or retains more of them; Harley-Davidson
- Capital; no one else has as much money; the major national and regional telecommunications companies
- Markets; no one else has access to a certain group of customers; American Express and other ultra-premium credit cards
- Strategic partners; no one else can leverage as many cooperative relationships; L.L. Bean
- Product quality; no one else makes as good a product or delivers a service as well; the Ritz-Carlton
- Process and systems; no one else possesses the efficiencies and flexibility; FedEx
- Marketing/sales; no one else is better at taking the product to market; the marketing power of the major international beverage (beer, water, soft drinks) manufacturers
- Cost controls/expense management; no one else can deliver the product more cost effectively; Wal-Mart
- People; no one else's employees are as resourceful or motivated; Disney

An obvious reaction after reading the list is that few if any companies possess even one of the characteristics as defined, and certainly no one company has them all. It would be great to be a "winner" with just one.

UNIQUENESS CHARACTERISTIC ASSESSMENT

Table 3.2 Uniquenes Characteristic Assessment

Totally Disagree 1	Somewhat Disagree 2	Don't know 3	Somewhat Agree 4	Totally Agree 5

1. The product itself . . . something no one else has

Totally Disagree	Somewhat Disagree	Don't know Not Applicable	Somewhat Agree	Totally Agree

2. Capital . . . no one else has as much money

Totally Disagree	Somewhat Disagree	Don't know Not Applicable	Somewhat Agree	Totally Agree

3. Markets . . . no one else has access to a certain group of customers

Totally Disagree	Somewhat Disagree	Don't know Not Applicable	Somewhat Agree	Totally Agree

4. Strategic Partners . . . no one else can leverage as many cooperative relationships

Totally Disagree	Somewhat Disagree	Don't know Not Applicable	Somewhat Agree	Totally Agree

5. Product Quality . . . no one else makes as good a product or delivers a service as well

Totally Disagree	Somewhat Disagree	Don't know Not Applicable	Somewhat Agree	Totally Agree

6. Customer Support . . . no one else takes better care of the customers

Totally Disagree	Somewhat Disagree	Don't know Not Applicable	Somewhat Agree	Totally Agree

7. Price . . . no one else offers similar value at a lower price

Totally Disagree	Somewhat Disagree	Don't know Not Applicable	Somewhat Agree	Totally Agree

8. Process and systems . . . no one else possesses the efficiencies and flexibility

Totally Disagree	Somewhat Disagree	Don't know Not Applicable	Somewhat Agree	Totally Agree

Table 3.2 (*Continued*)

9. Marketing/Sales . . . no one else is better at taking the product/service to market

Totally Disagree	Somewhat Disagree	Don't know Not Applicable	Somewhat Agree	Totally Agree

10. Cost controls/expense management . . . no one else can produce the product or deliver the service more cost-effectively

Totally Disagree	Somewhat Disagree	Don't know Not Applicable	Somewhat Agree	Totally Agree

11. People . . . no one else's employees are as resourceful or motivated

Totally Disagree	Somewhat Disagree	Don't know Not Applicable	Somewhat Agree	Totally Agree

A few observations of the ratings you gave yourself:

- As the questions are phrased, if you have any "5's," you have found your uniqueness! A "5" means nobody has it or does it better than your company.
- Too many "3's" indicate that you are not in a position to create a meaningful value proposition.
- Too many "1's" indicate that you have no uniqueness and need to reassess the business plan.
- Hopefully, you will come up with a few "4's." The "4's" indicate your company's existing and/or emerging uniqueness characteristics and will form the basis for your value proposition.

SUMMARY

The ratings are fun to do and help managers develop a higher awareness and new perspectives. But, in order to sustain profitable growth, companies must know what they are good at and how those competencies translate into well-founded value propositions. Value propositions are meaningless, and worse, potentially delusional, unless they present an accurate and realistic assessment of what the company can deliver.

A company must answer three simple questions.

- *Why should customers buy from us?*
- *Why should investors invest in us?*
- *Why should employees remain with us?*

YOUR NICHE

This section addresses the second critical planning element, your niche. The basics regarding targeting and niche identification are briefly reviewed. But, the emphasis focuses on two niche-related issues particularly relevant to growth companies: the Any Customer is a Good Customer syndrome and the the Allure of New Niches. But first, a few basics.

Niche 101

Companies intuitively understand the importance of identifying the most lucrative segment of the market; the one to which the company can deliver the most value, the one that most closely matches the company's ability to serve, the one with needs and wants the company can satisfy better than the competition. That can all be summarized by asking two questions: Who are your customers? and why have they been attracted to your product or service?

Niches evolve in start-up companies. More about that in a moment. However, once the company starts to grow, it begins to conduct basic analysis on its customers and prospects. The analysis takes various forms, but is fundamentally a three-step process:

- Assess the company's capabilities to serve (product offerings, support capabilities, marketing savvy, etc.) and determine the characteristics of potential customers that are most likely to buy the product/service.
- Identify as precisely as possible who those potential customers are.
- Prioritize potential customers based on their ability to buy and the company's ability to provide the desired product or service.

For example, XYZ Corporation knows that it makes expensive, upper-end sunglasses that offer features and benefits to potential customers who have the purchasing power and perceived need for high-fashion eyewear. XYZ identifies those prospects who meet the criteria: the ability to buy and perceived need. Then, based on other factors such as production and distribution capabilities, XYZ concludes that females over thirty, in households with income over $125,000 a year, who are employed and live in the Midwest are the top priority.

After that, the art and science of segmentation and targeting take over and will become more sophisticated as the company grows. It all starts with those three steps. Ultimately, segmentation and targeting competencies should become major strategic assets for the company.

So, the conclusion of three quick paragraphs on segmentation and targeting: begin as soon as possible; do them well; constantly improve in order to turn them into strategic advantages.

"Any Customer Is a Good Customer"

In chapter 6 we write at length about the importance of customer profitability. However, the subject cannot be ignored in any niche discussion, so we offer a brief explanation here.

In the entrepreneurial stage, many companies adhere to an entirely logical theory: "any customer is a good customer." During that stage, when growth of revenue and cash flow are paramount, it makes perfectly good sense. The business plan certainly identified a "target market" (examples: small businesses in major MSAs in the mid-Atlantic region, or upper-income consumers over fifty-five years old, or industrial distributors with over $5 million in annual revenues, etc.) After all, any business plan worth the paper it's written on must wax eloquently about its "target market." In reality, although, the company may focus on the "target" market to one degree or another, it is likely that several factors will divert the company from its original course:

- The target market analysis was incomplete or flawed to begin with.
- The environment and/or the company changed so rapidly that the original assumptions that identified the original target market become obsolete.
- Tactical financial pressures force a voluntary or involuntary broadening of the target market's definition.
- The sales organization (typically the dominant function in the entrepreneurial stage) pressures management to expand the target market definition in order to "create more opportunities."

With those factors in play, the company's natural niche begins to evolve on its own. The company finds its selling efforts are much more successful with some customer groups than others. The evolving niche will display certain characteristics:

- Lower sales costs
- Higher close ratios
- Higher margins
- Higher customer retention

- Higher add-on sales
- More repeat buyers

And, the emerging niche defines itself along one or more dimensions:

- The customers' needs
- Customer size
- The customers' demographic profile (B2C) or industry (B2B).
- Geography
- Some natural affinity to the company's product portfolio

The company begins to notice who its preferred customers are and codifies its business rules to drive sales channels to that niche. Product development focuses on what that niche needs and wants. Sales compensation plans and incentives drive the desired selling behaviors. The whole company focuses on what now has become its selected niche.

In a service company with which we are familiar, the original target market included midsize business customers who had multiple locations. The rationale seemed sound: higher revenue, one decision-maker for several locations, a certain amount of prestige to be gained serving these types of customers, the need to field only a moderately sized sales force.

However, for many reasons (some of which are detailed in chapter 6), the company found that the targeted segment was simply not working. Not without significant disruption, the company learned that single-location small businesses were much better suited for its products and support capabilities, so the targeted niche redefined itself.

Though things seem to be moving along swimmingly, a growth company is forced to deal with "baggage" from the past. It is inevitable because, remember, not too many months or years ago it believed that "any customer is a good customer."

Firing Customers?!?!? As growth companies more clearly define their niche, they soon see that many of their existing customers do not fit. Some portion of the existing base, when compared to the newly re-fined niche, pose problems and issues that must be dealt with. These "legacy" customers share one or more of the following characteristics when compared to the targeted niche customers:

- Lower margins
- Higher sales/marketing costs
- Costly, more specialized customer service

- "Nonstandard" systems requirements
- Expensive support capabilities for now obsolete products

A large number of "legacy" customers have a negative financial impact on the company. However, perhaps more threatening, they require a disproportionate amount of management's mindshare. These resources could and should be turning their attention to the newly defined niche in order to fully exploit the potential it offers. The previously mentioned service company is a case in point. The larger customers had more complex support requirements than the company could provide. They were sophisticated enough to demand (and receive) discounts that led to low profitability. And, they literally felt no hesitation in picking up the phone and calling senior management anytime anything didn't go their way.

The same phenomenon occurs in the consumer market. Department stores have found that a small percentage of their customers account for the vast majority of returns. Though the demographics of these buyers may correlate with the targeted niche, the behaviors of some clearly make them undesirable.

For most executives, particularly those who vividly remember the start-up days, a completely counterintuitive decision must be made: Some customers need to be fired! There's no easy way to do it, but targeted price increases and/or reductions in support capabilities are justifiable when certain segments of the customer base do not meet the company's margin threshold.

This does not infer that legacy customers are bad people or that the company doesn't appreciate the business these customers provided early on. Because they came when the company really needed them, the decision to fire them is very difficult and sometimes emotional. However, making the tough call here is necessary. The company is at a stage where it requires every ounce of energy, time, and effort to grow ... and grow by attracting customers it can best serve.

For Goodness Sake, Don't Acquire Any New "Legacy" Customers Servicing new and legacy customers, when put together, sounds completely contradictory. However, as the company is fully defining and fleshing out its niche, it is highly probable that the sales force is busily acquiring new "legacy" customers. The new niche is not yet formalized, and compensation and motivation schemes date back to the "old days." Compensation and motivation programs still reflect the "any customer is a good customer" philosophy. So, the sales force is happily acquiring customers who are rapidly moving out of the company's "strike zone" ... and sales is being paid commissions and bonuses to do so.

Whether the company is removing legacy customers from its base or narrowing the market opportunity (as perceived by the sellers), by changing compensation schemes to support the new niche, it can count on serious push-back from the sales channels.

Niche changes that the company is making mark a literal shift in the power base within the company. The sales organization loses some of its historical power and autonomy; the remainder of the company acquires authority and more say-so in what the sellers do in terms of products offered, prospects targeted, prices charged, and compensation paid. Translation: The marketing function is born.

The reduction of the "legacy" customer base and stopping the acquisition of new "legacy" customers is a must, despite the inevitable protestations from the sellers.

The company should take great care in communicating its reasons for the change to the sales force. They have done absolutely nothing wrong. They were selling by the rules they were given. It's the company's responsibility to change the rules when necessary and clearly communicate the rationale. But, the last thing you want is a highly motivated and well-compensated sales force acquiring customers you really don't want.

We recall an industrial manufacturer that entered a market segment with a new product that performed very well. It was the company's "flagship" product for several years. However, new, more profitable products were introduced over time. And, several lawsuits were filed against the company when the "flagship" malfunctioned and caused several injuries.

Though the "flagship" was reengineered and was not an ongoing safety problem, it created a black eye for the firm. Even though more profitable products had been introduced, and management wanted to distance the company from the product until it could be withdrawn from the market . . . guess what?

Premium sales commissions were still being paid to the channels to move the tainted product. Hello!

More on this in chapter 6.

The Allure of New Niches

The previous section addressed challenges to implementing niche strategies as the company moves out of the entrepreneurial stage. However, once the company defines its niche and becomes successful marketing to it, a new temptation will creep into the picture: the allure of new niches.

Success should breed confidence. Profitable growth indicates that the company is not just lucky; it's doing things right and it's working.

Just as the company eliminates the niche "sins" of the past and begins to benefit from a well-defined niche strategy, someone poses the inevitable question: "You know, we're doing so well in Niche 1 we would be foolish not to seriously consider entering Niche 2." After all, high-growth companies must constantly look for new business opportunities. Right?

Absolutely, but there is a huge difference between sustaining growth within a niche and creating a new one. Companies must clearly understand the difference and not be enticed into entering new niches without careful due diligence and analysis.

Tom Peters called it "sticking to the knitting," and the phrase has as much import today as it did twenty years ago. "The allure of new niches" is closely akin to the "Any customer is a good customer" issue discussed earlier, however, now it's at a much more sophisticated level. The company is not being forced to attract customers outside its niche because it needs the revenue to make payroll, that's history; it wants to look at new niches for other reasons . . . some valid, some not.

Invalid reasons have to do with ego, smugness, arrogance, and over-confidence. Michael Jordan proved decisively that being the world's best basketball player meant nothing on the baseball diamond. His performance in a new niche was mediocre at best and he returned to his "knitting." However, his success in his primary niche was at such a high level that he could fall back on it with little damage . . . except a dent in his ego.

Growth companies usually don't have that luxury. A misguided adventure into new niches can, at best, stagger a company and set its growth plans back. At worst, it will kill a company.

A national industrial manufacturer had become a national leader in the manufacture and distribution of a certain product group; we'll call it product A. Product A was sold primarily to very large companies, usually through a direct sales force. It was a technologically sophisticated product, and almost all Product As sold were customized.

Senior management acquired another manufacturer that produced Product B. It bought the company, mostly for the value of its brand, and decided to manufacture Product B in its own factories, which had spare capacity. However, Product B was not technologically sophisticated and was distributed through third-party channels to rather unsophisticated buyers. It was a completely different product in every imaginable way from Product A.

The outcome: disaster. Whatever anticipated synergy and economies of scale that had been anticipated were overwhelmed by the problems brought on by the company's absolute lack of understanding of Product B's customers, distribution network, and marketing/sales requirements. Entering what seemed a logical expansion niche eventually led the company to withdraw from the Product B market.

An amazingly simple assessment can indicate whether or not a company is wasting its time thinking about entering a new niche. That assessment, which follows, guides the company in comparing the customer and competence requirements of its existing niche with those of a new one. It helps management quickly determine whether or not consideration of a new niche warrants the resources and analysis required.

When you complete the assessment, if 75 percent of the new niche's required competencies are not already resident in the company, pursuit of it will require massive amounts of time and money. Stated differently, if the company doesn't already know most of what it needs to know and already have the ability to do what it will need to do to be successful in the new niche, pursuing it will likely be extremely difficult and expensive.

New Niche Assessment

For each of the items in the left-hand column, briefly describe current knowledge and competencies for the existing niche. For the new niche, do the same. If there is not at least a 75 percent similarity

Table 3.3 New Niche Assessment

	Current Niche	**New Niche**
Customer Needs/Market Conditions		
Buying Criteria		
Support Requirements		
Product/Service Needs		
The Competition		
Company Competencies		
Market Knowledge		
Product Development		
Customer Support		
Process/Systems		
Production/Fulfillment		
Capital		
Cultural Fit		

between the two in each of the categories, seriously reconsider going after the new niche.

COMPETITIVE ANALYSIS: BIG FISH AND LITTLE FISH

Competitive information collection/analysis and strategy development is the third planning element singled out for special attention.

The competitive analysis and planning requirements in growth companies are, like everything else, in a constant state of change. Not only are competitors and the company constantly changing, the way the company views its competitors and how they view you are also nonstatic variables. This section looks at the changes going on in those three dimensions and suggests ways for the company to manage them successfully.

The Fish Analogy

In chapter 1 we looked at the four stages of company growth. Overlaying those are phases a company goes through in terms of how it assesses and is assessed by its competitors. The fundamental assumptions for this analogy are based on the fact that companies, as they grow and become more successful, must alter the ways they assess their competitors. Not only is the nature of the analysis different, but the company will identify different subgroups of competitors at different stages in its growth cycle. Some competitors that were consequential to the company during start-up become irrelevant. Similarly, competitors that were irrelevant early on become a major concern as the company grows. And, of course, competitors are always coming and going as a natural characteristic of the marketplace, with new entrants, mergers, bankruptcies, and the like.

Since the "stages of competition" may or may not directly correlate with the growth phases of the business, an aquatic analogy surfaces (pun intended) and is used to categorize both the company's and its competitors' evolution.

The Fish

The Minnow
- Company is likely in the entrepreneurial stage.
- It has no measurable market share.

- Its marketing practices have practically no impact in the marketplace.
- It is a "follower" desperately trying to find its niche.
- Surviving for another day dominates its existence.
- Major competitors have never heard of the company and could care less.

The Bream
- Company experiencing some growth.
- It is having some local or regional success.
- In those localized markets, its marketing efforts gain notice, but likely from other bream.
- Large competitors are still paying little attention, but small ones are beginning to take notice.

The Bass
- The company is relatively stable and experiencing significant regional growth.
- Its marketplace practices are noted by all competitors.
- Breams become intimidated.
- Barracudas start circling, trying to figure out what's going on.
- Even a Great White pays casual attention.

The Barracuda
- The company is well funded and has acquired significant cumulative experience.
- It has a strong regional and emerging national presence.
- It eats bream and bass for lunch in the marketplace.
- It is in constant battles with other barracudas and has the scars to prove it.

The Great White
- A dominant national and/or international player.
- Probably one of a relatively few number of trendsetters in the industry.
- Pretty much does what it wants to do when it wants to do it.
- Eats barracuda and a few bass in the marketplace; also eats a few for acquisition, too.

Size and Ferocity

No doubt you noted that the fish grow both in size and ferociousness. Not only do the fish get bigger, they develop an "attitude."

That's natural; with increasing size, companies gain the ability to throw their weight around and are not hesitant in doing so. They have bulk and capital. They have the confidence of success. And, to satiate the need for continued growth, they must develop an "attitude" in the marketplace. And, it's usually a lot safer and more productive to pick on fish their size or smaller.

Therein is the challenge for growth companies: knowing what kind of fish both they and their competitors are and developing plans to effectively cope with the anticipated actions of other fish, primarily the larger ones.

Who Pays Attention To Whom?

The following graphic illustrates the focus of competitive attention of the various "species."

Your Company's Perspective (The Vertical Ovals) As a minnow, you must be concerned about everybody! As the company defines its niche and value proposition, it is imperative that it have at least a cursory

Figure 3.1 Your Company's Species (& Your Interest in Other Species)

Your company	Minnow	Bream	Bass	Barracuda	Great White
The Competitor's Species (Their interest in you)					
Minnow					
Bream					
Bass					
Barracuda					
Great White					

understanding of what its competitors are doing...doing well and doing poorly. Ironically, this is the time when the company has the fewest resources, and the assessment is usually limited to basic product and price information.

As a bream, the company is less interested in what the minnows are doing and focuses on competitors that are the same size and larger. The company's analytical capabilities grow but are concentrated on a smaller number of competitors. This trend continues as the company becomes a bass.

The barracuda company not only assesses larger competitors, but because of its growing appetite it expands its view back down the food chain to weaker competitors. Should it ever become a great white, the company will develop complete portfolios on every competitor in the marketplace. When your company reaches the barracuda or great white stage, it should not make the mistake of ignoring the bream and bass...something many larger companies did, which was a major contributor to your current success.

The Competitors' Perspective (The Horizontal Ovals) As a minnow, few substantial competitors know or care about what you are doing. Other minnows are in the same position and react tactically to you in local markets.

The larger fish begin to pay more attention to you (if they're smart). The company will attract their attention. The more successful you are, the more attention you receive. In some perverse way it is flattering when larger fish notice you on their radar screens, but it goes without saying that, whatever flattery may be felt, significant and effective initiatives directed toward you by larger fish will have a huge impact on the company.

Evolving Competitive Analyses

Developing effective strategies to deal with the moving parts (or swimming fish) is dependent on a constantly evolving competitive analysis process. What you don't know, you can't plan countermeasures for; and, it can kill you!

The following exercise allows you to plot your company's competitive information collection and analyze its competitive competence. The company's vision of the importance of competitive intelligence, the actual "database" of competitive information, and the analytical process used to develop strategy must become more comprehensive with growth.

COMPETITIVE ANALYSIS EVOLUTION

Table 3.4 Competitive Analysis Evolution

'From'	1	2	3	4	5	'To'
Reactive						Proactive
Survivor mind-set						Predator mind-set
Competitive knowledge						Competitive analysis
Focused on competitors' product, price						Focused on competitors' strategies
Focused on what competitors *have done*						Focused on what competitors *will do*
Product/service competition						Total value competition
Sales/marketing focus						Total company focus

There is no "passing" score threshold per se. Companies at different growth stages have different needs and capabilities. However, as a rule of thumb, if the point total does not exceed 25, it is unlikely that the company's competitive analysis and strategy development are postured for sustained profitable growth.

There Are Always Larger Fish; There Are Always Smaller Fish

Unless your company is the great white in your market, smaller and larger competitors exist. All the fish species have their own particular competitive strengths and weaknesses. Small fish are more agile and flexible. Larger fish have more resources and market clout. So, no matter what type of fish your company is or will become, there are fish out there that have distinct competitive advantages over you.

Learning, in detail, what those advantages are and reassessing them continually is a planning imperative. They are constantly changing, as is your company. What was an advantage today may be a disadvantage tomorrow. Of all the variables resident in a company's planning process, none is more dynamic than the company's competitive position in the marketplace. None deserves more continuing attention.

THE EXIT STRATEGY

This is a short section about a term; but it addresses a subtlety that has tangible and intangible implications for a growth company.

We personally find the term "exit strategy" distasteful, inappropriate, and misleading...its one that has absolutely no place in a growth company. Perhaps our objection to the term is based on semantics, but nonetheless, it should be banned from your vocabulary.

Who's Exiting What?

- Is the company exiting the industry?
- Is the company exiting doing business?
- Are the executives exiting the company?
- Is the company exiting the town?
- Are the investors exiting?

We have observed that companies use the term with appalling regularity in business plans and, worse, public forums. By its very nature, "exit strategy" infers a lack of permanence and a preordained conclusion. Though exceptions exist, the vast majority of growth companies intend to remain viable, ongoing enterprises. To suggest otherwise is counterintuitive to the concept of "growth."

Mergers, acquisitions, and buyouts occur. So do bankruptcies (certainly an exit event). However, firms that, from the outset, plan for their eventual dissolution do not qualify by our definition as viable growth companies. They are not growth companies; they are "temporary" companies. Real growth companies cannot maximize their potential by planning for the day they will not exist. Financiers may have their own exit strategy, but the company cannot.

Implications

There is nothing wrong with a temporary company as long as it's not passed off as a growth company. The cognitive dissonance that resonates through the company's constituencies drives them all to madness. If a company is temporary, say so, and plan and execute accordingly.

Intellectual honesty and clarity in communications are mandatory. If a company is truly growth-oriented and committed to permanence, it should avoid having an "exit strategy." Implications of not doing so are real.

Strategic focus will be diluted. If the management team as a whole or any individual is focused on something other than long term viability and prosperity, the energy and focus required for such becomes fragmented.

Infrastructure will be shortchanged. If there are any lingering doubts that
the company is not in it for the "long haul," shortcuts are taken and
infrastructure for sustained growth is not deployed. After all, "why
spend the money, we'll be out of this thing in eighteen months."

Employees will not remain fully committed. Once the employee base perceives this temporariness, they think and act like temporary employees. Your customers are the first to experience the employees'
change in attitude.

Having an "exit strategy" is okay for temporary companies, but it
has no place in growth companies.

COST-CUTTING: THE EBB AND FLOW OF ABSURDITY

If it hasn't happened yet, it soon will. A company's growth curve is
never smooth nor always positive. Any number of factors will periodically slow growth; maybe even cause negative growth for a period
of time. And then, the inevitable occurs: "It's cost-cutting time."

Why Do You Need to Cut Costs?

Because they are too high, but how did they get that way? Good
reasons include the buildup of personnel and infrastructure to support more and more customers. If sales go down and the customer
base becomes smaller, it is logical and prudent to reduce the associated costs. A bad reason why costs are too high is frivolous expenses
that create no value for the company somehow slipped into the budget
during the "good times."

Regrettably, when cost-cutting comes, it is done under duress
and possibly with a sense of panic. That's particularly the case if the
turndown is the first the company has experienced. To use an analogy,
management brings out the shotgun rather than the rifle and starts
blasting away.

Budget Creep: A Familiar Story?

The natural frugality of the company in the entrepreneurial stage
was a requisite for survival. Capital was limited, and managing the
company's finances as if they were one's personal checking account
(sometimes it was) was not unusual.

There was an intense focus on cash. Whether the founders were financing the company themselves and/or with outside capital, every expenditure was scrutinized. There was little room for waste and every penny was accounted for.

During this early growth spurt, many expenditures once considered optional were funded, with many of them necessary and certainly not considered "luxuries." Needed staff additions once unaffordable were funded. Bare-boned promotional programs were beefed up. And, compensation for key employees became commensurate with their contributions to the business.

These are valid "catch-up" expenditures, and there are many more like them. However, at what point were the valid, previously nonfunded or underfunded activities brought up to par, and when did nonmission critical expenditures make their way into the budget?

There was not a "magic moment." It was a gradual and normal process that accompanies success. Expenditures became entrenched. They had been in the budget for a year or two and were not scrutinized. They became customary and accepted.

A year or two ago the expenditure might have been very small, but it gradually increased. As the company grew, self-perpetuating bureaucracies developed and fabricated dozens of reasons why they needed not only to survive but grow. The focused attention that all expenditures once received became obfuscated by endless budget meetings and spreadsheet iterations.

Then, sales and revenues dropped, and mandated budget cuts were imposed. However, not all irrelevant line items were eliminated. Some survived at the expense of critical items because everyone was forced to "share the burden." Translation: It's easy to mandate across-the-board budget cuts; it's much more difficult to ferret out superfluous costs and eliminate them altogether while leaving mission-critical activities fully funded.

Targeted, Intelligent Cost-Cutting

When it's time to cut costs, growth companies must take a more sophisticated approach than their smaller and much larger brethren. The company has built an infrastructure and competencies that must not be squandered with the blind use of the budget ax. No one wants their ox gored, but, frankly, some oxen need goring more than others. With that in mind, following are the recommended steps management should follow to cut costs without "gutting" the company's ability to reenergize itself when times get better.

Introductory Meeting

- The senior and middle management teams meet and the cost-cutting goals are announced to all.
- The teams agree to support the corporate reduction goal.
- Officers and their directors are requested to submit a revised budget for the planning period.
- There is no mandated percent decrease.
- There are no "sacred cows"; everything is in play.
- Each organization is requested to develop substantiation for every line item.
- Budget *increases* will be entertained if they can be justified.
- The line item substantiation must include a "statement of necessity and value" that details the need for the expenditure in specific terms.
- Each department will prioritize its expenditures.
- Time frames are established and agreed upon.
- The funding meeting agenda is defined. Each participant will have an allotted time period to present the revised budget and answer questions.

Funding Meeting

- The presentations are made.
- No decisions are made regarding anyone's budget during the presentations.
- The CFO "keeps score" and revises the corporate budget with each presenter's suggested changes.
- When the presentations conclude, the CFO announces the collective impact of the recommended changes on the corporate budget.
- If the reductions are achieved, the meeting is over.
- If not, the team sets a time limit for further discussions, and negotiations continue until reductions are agreed to.
- At no time are "across the board" reductions discussed.

A few words of caution. The atmosphere in the funding meeting will be tense, and emotions may run high. The process creates intense pressure for everyone to "have their act together." The collective judgment of the team must be effective in separating substance from style. Teamwork principles described in a later chapter must be present in spades, and the team leader must bring out the best of everyone's desire to preserve the company's well-being.

Budget Reduction Truisms

The process's effectiveness is enhanced by keeping the following in mind:

- Senior management must be fully engaged in the process and its implementation.
- Delegation is not an option.
- The formality of the process is necessary.
- Specific implementation plans and time frames must be developed.
- Progress made on the implementation plans must be monitored and reported.
- Earnest and effective participation in the funding meeting and successful implementation of the new plans are part of everyone's performance evaluation.

Budget cuts are painful and difficult to deal with. But they are a natural part of "growing up." The pain can be made short-term by effective remedies. Or it can evolve into a chronic condition, bringing misery to the company far into the future. A company that must cut its budget but fully intends to reestablish its growth trajectory must be mindful not to administer a budget reduction "cure" that can permanently harm the "patient."

LINKING THE PLAN, THE BUDGET, THE BEHAVIORS

Growth companies, like most others, face several challenges when developing a budget. They include:

- Effectively integrating the budgeting process with the company's plans and strategies.
- Since strategies drive budgets, budgets drive compensation and compensation drives behaviors, insuring that all are aligned to obtain the desired results.
- Building a budget that reflects the dynamic environment in which growth companies exist; not just "warming over" last year's version.

Integration

One would be surprised by the number of companies that do not relate their strategic planning process to their budgeting. The primary reason stems from the ancient malady of viewing planning as some sort of mystic process that's unrelated to the "real world." Maybe finance has always developed the budget, looking at what happened in the past and extrapolating it to represent the future. Or perhaps little or no planning existed historically, and there is little faith in the strategic planning process and its outputs.

Whatever the cause, a plan, no matter how credible, is completely meaningless if it is not the sole driver of the budgeting process. If the budget is not "linked at the hip" to the plan, it is focused on the past. Relatively arbitrary estimates of percent increase in sales and the commensurate increase in expenses do not reflect the changing environment, as the strategic plan does, or should. New competitors enter the market. New products are rolled out. Everything is in flux in a growth company. How can any budget be of value if it is founded on what has already happened?

An astronomy analogy comes to mind. Deep space researchers "see" what actually occurred billions of years ago. Backward-looking budgeting "sees" what happened one or two years ago, and the numbers that are put into the spreadsheet are hopelessly dated the moment the file is saved.

Budgets and Behaviors

Several years ago a large technology manufacturer got into trouble when its sales organization "booked" millions of dollars in sales long before the deals were actually closed. And we are familiar with shady arrangements with suppliers where they accelerate or delay billing based on the buyer's desire to have the expenses fall in one budget period or another.

Behaviors like these are usually driven by incentives that originate in the budgeting process. Some are unethical or illegal; most are the manipulations of a "system" that encourages minor league hanky-panky. This sort of foolishness cannot be avoided altogether, but a company's budgeting process, if properly designed and implemented, can and will reduce the need and temptation for "beating the system."

The Remedy: The CASB Process

CASB (customer acquisition/support budgeting) is a budgeting regimen built around those activities directly associated with acquiring and retaining customers. CASB adopts the principles of the ABC and REM theories (see chapter 6) and overlays zero-based budgeting fundamentals, something you probably recognized in the cost-cutting section. But more important, it demands the direct and complete linkage of the budgeting process to the company's planning. The process is diagrammed at the end of the chapter as a reference.

CASB Overview CASB assumes that the company engages in high-quality strategic planning and that the process produces meaningful quantitative and qualitative goals and objectives. These fall into three categories:

- Customer acquisition and support
- Financial performance measures
- Corporate overheads

CAS (Customer Acquisition and Support) Originating directly from the strategic plan, CAS identifies the revenue expectations for the upcoming period (acquisition) as well as customer support requirements for new sales and the existing base. The sales organization forecasts unit volumes at a detailed level and communicates them to marketing, operations, Information Technology/Management Information System (IT/MIS), and human resources. These organizations create departmental budgets required to support the forecasted sales volume and existing customer base. All the department budgets are aggregated in the consolidated CAS budget.

The CAS budget identifies all revenues for the company and the costs that are directly related to acquiring and supporting customers. Those expenses include:

- Purchasing/production: cost of goods sold (COGS)
- Sales: Direct and indirect sales expenses
- Marketing: Product management, advertising promotion, research, etc.
- Operations: Fulfillment/production, customer service/support
- IT/MIS: discrete expenses in support of purchasing, sales, marketing, and operations (work stations, etc.)
- Human resources: Recruiting, training for purchasing, sales, marketing, and operations employees

The CAS sub-budget captures all expenses that are associated with sales activities and the existing customer base. The relationship between customers and their associated revenues and expenses provides a benchmark for productivity and focus on an ongoing basis.

Financial Performance Goals The strategic plan clearly identifies the key financial goals of the company for the planning period. The sales/revenue goal is working its way through the CAS process and the corporate overhead budget is being developed. However, independent of those two processes, senior management establishes additional preliminary goals for the company; revenue, profitability, Return on Equity (ROE), and so on.

Corporate Overhead Budget Forecast Simultaneous to the CAS planning, the company's expenses not directly related to CAS are forecasted. These include 1) core corporate overheads that should not be allocated in the CAS process such as officer compensation, capital lease costs, interest expenses, etc.; 2) CAS-related costs that can't be easily allocated such as telecommunications/network expenses, and 3) costs for strategic initiatives such as legal/consulting expenses and actual costs of acquisitions.

Development of the Corporate Budget Once the three independent planning activities are completed, the senior team compiles the projected revenues and expenses from all sources, crunches the numbers, and compares the outcome with the preliminary corporate goals.

The Zero-Based Budgeting Overlay

CASB, though not expressly using the term, assumes that the company adopts a zero-based budgeting philosophy. That is, with the exception of the revenue goal, nothing else is provided in terms of budget guidance. All expenses are reset at "zero," and all requested expenditures are considered as "new" and must be justified.

CAS encourages the business acquisition and customer support departments to first build the sales/retention plan required to achieve the revenue objective and second, determine how it will be supported. There is no "maximum X percent increase in expenses allowed" directive. Nor is a "head count freeze" mandated. CAS places no constraints on teams as they develop their budgets.

A cynic might say that this sort of unguided approach will produce havoc. Departments will pad their budgets and ask for the moon. We disagree. The teams are smart; they know the company's past expectations and performance. And, they are each led by a member of the senior team. The creativity and thoughtfulness the teams will exhibit might be surprising if given the latitude.

A more direct approach is suggested for forecasting corporate expenses. As indicated earlier, much of the "fat" that may have crept into the budget resides in "corporate." Corporate expenses should be zero-based; that is, the protocol that was suggested for dealing with budget cuts in the earlier section should be implemented when developing the corporate budget. The initial assumption: Nothing is budgeted; justify what's needed based on the strategic plan, not on what was spent last year.

We cannot emphasize enough how effective such an approach is in flushing out unnecessary spending. Unlike the fiscal behaviors of our federal government, where nothing is ever cut from the budget, and the bureaucrats yelp whenever there is a *decrease in the growth*

Figure 3.2 Customer Acquisition, Support, and Budgeting Process (CASB)

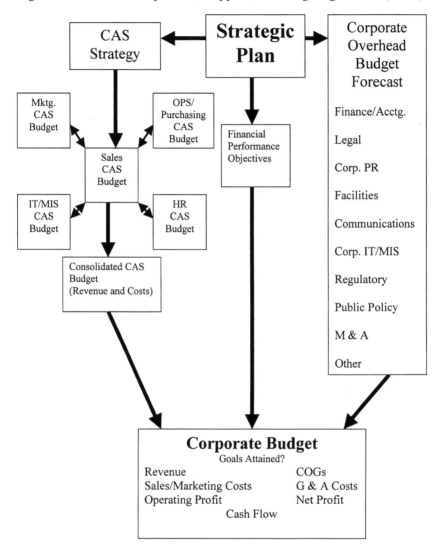

rate of the increase in spending, savvy growth companies simply cannot afford the same luxury. When *every* expense, legacy or otherwise, must be justified, human nature takes over. The threat of scrutiny will change behavior. Expenses will go down.

Be hard-nosed before you are forced to be!

Budget Adjustments

Many growth companies do not use a traditional annual budgeting process. They find the world in which they live too dynamic to accurately forecast twelve months in advance. A firm budget may be developed on a quarterly or six-month basis, with adjustments made periodically based on results and changing conditions. This is usually coupled with a "rolling" twelve-month planning budget and a two to three-year budget projection. These approaches are highly recommended.

The idea that a growth company can accurately forecast how many call center representatives will be required eleven months from now is ludicrous. Running the numbers based on sales forecasts and the anticipated level of customer calls makes sense . . . it forms a baseline; but assuming the forecasted number of reps will become an actual reality in eleven months is an exercise in self-delusion.

CASB, like any budgeting process, should generate an annual budget with longer-term projections. They form a meaningful baseline. However, we recommend that growth companies utilize the "quarterly timeouts" explained in an earlier section as the proper forum to review and firm up the next couple of quarters. The quarterly timeouts are scheduled reassessments of data and assumptions that led to strategy development. If these facts or assumptions change, the strategies must be adjusted. If the strategies readjust, so should the budget.

When the three planning elements come together in the corporate budget, not all the pieces will fit. Not all the corporate goals will be met. The budget is a living and breathing document that must change as the company and environment changes. Those are realities. But, a budgeting process that is strategically driven and flexible is a mandatory requirement for growth companies.

Chapter 4

EXECUTING THE
BUSINESS PLAN

THE PLANNING RETREAT IS OVER!

Okay. The planning retreat is over and it was an outstanding success. Everyone was deliberate in their preparation and completely focused on the task at hand. All pettiness and departmental agendas were put aside, and for three days the management team put intense effort into realistically assessing the company and its environment. There was creative brainstorming, but no one went off the deep end and wasted valuable time on irrelevant issues. The facilitator was well prepared and did her homework as well.

Assumptions were tested and verified. Competitive intelligence was on-point, accurate, and in-depth. No "sacred cows" surfaced, so a meaningful and honest appraisal of the company's competencies and shortcomings was made. Most important, sound strategies and plans emerged. Everyone was pleased with the results and couldn't wait to get back to the office and get started.

What happens now to insure that the business follows the plan it has just spent so much time and effort developing?

Beware of the "Morning After" Syndrome

We're sure that every reader has attended motivational seminars or some other "attitude adjustment" sessions. The theories presented make so much sense and create wonderment as to why you hadn't thought of them long ago. Prejudices and blind spots are removed, and you leave the session enlightened. For a day or two you enthusiastically discuss the session with anyone who will listen and vow to use the new perspectives gained.

Then a business crisis jerks you back to reality, and those amazing insights of just a day or two ago become as dim as they were once vivid. A great planning session suffers the same plight as the motivational session unless management is committed to the ongoing execution of the plan. There is a major difference, however. A talented executive will not fail due to a forgotten motivational principle. However, a growth company with a promising future will not realize that promise if it "forgets" the plan.

Without management's commitment to effective, consistent execution, the plan languishes and never realizes even a small percentage of its potential. Writing a good plan accounts for, at best, 10 percent of success. Effective execution delivers the other 90 percent.

Selling the Plan

"Selling" the plan may be foreign to the management team. Everyone played a role in its creation and others in the organization provided input. The plan is documented, well written, and available to everyone. All the company needs now is for the management team to simply implement it, right? Not really, if the company wants to realize the full potential of the plan.

The Board Our observations of boards, particularly those of growth companies, are that they vary greatly in almost all the dimensions of business experience and acumen, industry knowledge, and degree of interest in the company. Most important, they may not share a common vision of the company's future. Depending on the board's dynamics and the company's evolution, there may be less consensus about the company's future than the management team realizes.

A detailed, formal presentation to the board accomplishes many objectives. It:

- Draws out any differing perspectives and forces needed discussion and consensus.
- Documents the company's direction and defines the expectations of senior management.
- Supplies supporting background information and rationale for financial decisions the board will make during the planning period.
- Allows the board to pose questions and concerns about the company's strategies before they are implemented.
- And, most important, it places the board and senior management on the same team. A high-growth company requires unanimity and unqualified support.

Middle Management Senior management is more and more dependent on middle management to run the company's day-to-day operations. The executives must completely embrace the fact that middle managers are more than mere task workers charged with implementing the plan handed down from above. They operate the company daily, and deserve much more than being handed a copy of the plan.

Middle management will also provide many of the leaders of the company in a few years. Growth and executive attrition creates opportunities, many of which will be filled by existing middle management. They should be considered senior managers in waiting and integrated into the planning and execution as much as is plausible and feasible.

We recommend that senior management present the plan to their middle managers with the same professionalism and content as was provided to the board. Middle management's understanding and support of the plan is as crucial as that of the board. You are asking a lot of your middle management, and most of them are capable of delivering, but only if fully informed of the company's direction and the roles you want them to play.

Employees The employee base wants to understand what their employer's plans are. Of course, the full content of the plan cannot and should not be shared with all of the employees. However, to expect the employees to be committed to what is asked of them, they need to know where the company is going.

The senior team should present a relevant synopsis of the plan and provide updates as appropriate. As we will address in chapter 5, leaders must appeal equally effectively to the followers' hearts and minds. Company picnics and a nourishing work environment will soothe the heart. A concise explanation of where the company is going and how it intends to get there invigorates the mind.

Key Linkages

Four fundamental threads weave the plan into the operations of the business and facilitate its execution. Without these linkages, successful plan execution is all but impossible.

The Marketing and Operations Plans Marketing and Operations Plans are those formal and quasi-formal planning activities that bring granularity to the strategies developed at the corporate level. Though technically considered planning activities, they build the bridge between the corporate plan and tactical departmental activities. Without that bridge, growing companies find overall execution difficult. During start-up, the leap between the corporate plan and daily tactics was easy to make, but with the complexities of growth, the gap widens. Therefore, "fleshing out" the corporate plan in the form of details of just how the company will acquire/retain customers and produce its products and services (Marketing and Operations Plans) becomes a step necessary for successful execution.

The Budget Though the case for planning and budgeting integration was made in an earlier chapter, we reiterate their primary function: to quantify the activities defined by the company's plans and document progress made. How many times have you heard "It's time to do next year's budget," or "We've got to make some changes in the budget." Those statements are analogous to posting the final score of the football game on the scoreboard before the third quarter is over. A company creates or modifies plans, not budgets. Budgets document all the financial elements of the plan; they are necessary and integral parts of running the business. Budgets report on the business; they don't guide it. Good plans do.

Metrics Some sage once said something to the effect that "It's not worth doing if it can't be measured." Another added, "What gets measured gets managed." Most agree that metrics should be used to bring attention to the activities the company deems relevant and important. Those activities must originate in the plan and support the objectives defined by the plan. Metrics are linked to compensation throughout the company; therefore, the company must be mindful that behaviors will be focused on the achievement of metrics. Linkage must exist between the plan and the metrics. Otherwise, the company does not create the desired emphasis and/or inadvertently emphasizes the irrelevant.

Organizational Structure/Resource Allocation The organizational structure of the company must be aligned with the plans it is tasked with executing. The structure itself must reflect the activities that are in the plan. If the plan calls for increased market/competitive analyses and the function does not currently exist, obviously it must be created. If interdepartmental task forces are required, the reporting relationships must be adjusted to support them. Resources, human and otherwise, must be aligned to support the plan. Marginal activities that are not germane to the plan's priorities must be scrutinized.

So, to summarize:

- Marketing and Operations Plans bring planning down to ground level, down from fifty thousand feet where the strategists dwell; who's going to do what by when?

- The budget is built to fund those Marketing and Operations Plans that have been approved; these plans will be developed in enough detail to insure that budgeting is a meaningful exercise.
- Metrics identify those activities in the Strategic, Marketing, and Operations Plans that will be measured and specifically define what a satisfactory level of performance will be.
- Then, management must insure that the company is organized from top to bottom in a way that is consistent with the successful implementation of the approved plans.

PLAIN OLD FOLLOW-THROUGH

"Quarterly timeouts" were recommended in chapter 3, quarterly semiformal reassessments of the plan. However, effective execution is dependent on the plan being part and parcel of how business is conducted every day.

- Copies of the plan (sans sensitive data) should be on every senior and middle manager's desk. It should be well-worn, dog-eared, and full of notes and comments.
- Executives and managers should bring it to every staff meeting. The plan should guide execution day in and day out. Pedestrian problems, opportunities, and issues should be "bounced off" the plan.
- Status reports on progress being made (per the plan, not just the budget) should be a permanent agenda item in board meetings.
- Progress reports should also become a part of employee communications programs.

Execution is defined simply as putting the plan to work. Significant company resources are devoted to the development of the plan. The plan is the road map to guide the company's activities. It must be allowed to do so.

MANAGING THE MOTHER OF ALL BALANCING ACTS: CHAOS VERSUS BUREAUCRACY

Growing companies are inevitably faced with the challenge of putting business processes in place, those command and control elements essential in dealing with the ever-increasing size and complexity of the business. The company is constantly faced with answering nagging questions:

- How much process is enough?
- How do we retain the agility and flexibility of entrepreneurship?
- What is the point where process becomes bureaucracy?
- How do we know when process development becomes an end unto itself rather than a necessary element in the maturity of the business?

Answering these questions is a constant and ongoing judgment call as the company grows. There are no pat answers, but developing structure in a growth company, in the proper amount, is one of the most challenging tasks facing senior management.

The Early Days

The company's emphasis or lack of it on process, planning and organizing, and command and control originated in the personalities of the founders. If they placed importance on process, the company possessed such an orientation from the very beginning. However, that would be an unusual scenario.

By definition, entrepreneurs do not place a premium on process development. At the risk of reinforcing a stereotype, it is safe to say that most entrepreneurs excel at decision-making, making intuitive judgments, making the most from nothing, and passing along enthusiasm and passion for the company. But, most don't wake up in the morning worrying about process development.

A business process can be defined as a predetermined series of activities governing the interaction among employees or between the company's employees and its vendors, its customers, or other constituencies. Examples include new product introduction; recruiting, interviewing, and selection; complaint resolution and recovery; order entry/fulfillment; claims processing; and so on. Some entrepreneurs are not only ambivalent toward process development, some find it constraining and inhibiting. Others may view it as a threat to the flexibility they feel they need and will consciously retard its development. It's not logical, but it happens.

Additionally, during start-up, companies have precious few resources to spend on process. The business is simple enough at that stage, and capital and effort are better expended on much higher priorities. And, the employee body is so small that word-of-mouth and on-the-job training (OJT) were effective in passing along "how it's done" to new employees. Senior management was readily available to make decisions regarding even the smallest issues. Things got done and got done rather effectively.

Therefore, most companies exiting the entrepreneurial stage have minimum processes in place. Process development was a low/no priority, and the lack of it really didn't cause any problems. But that's about to change.

Growth and Process

As the company begins to grow, so does process development, whether or not management realizes it. Process-minded employees develop ad hoc departmental procedures, usually in the form of aids for training new hires.

Without corporate direction, uncoordinated and departmental-specific procedures evolve. If one vice president makes it a priority in his organization, process development evolves very quickly. In a department where the vice president has not made process development a priority, little is done. Soon conflicts develop among departments that are focused on process and those that are not. And, they can become vicious little battles. Interdepartmental squabbles regarding process are likely the impetus for the company, as a whole, to step up to the process development challenge.

Whatever the motivating factor, the company's senior management team must tackle the process development issue before the company's operation slowly grinds to a halt. The team must also realize that processes forever alter the way the company does business. The old "do what feels good" and "just use your best judgment" approaches are now obsolete.

PROCESS DEVELOPMENT CHECKLIST

The following list of business processes is by no means inclusive. Different companies and different industries require unique processes. However, the list does address many universal business activities and will assist management in determining where the company currently stands and in identifying future priorities for process development.

Existing Processes

1 = nonexistent/don't know
2 = minimal
3 = partly in place
4 = substantially in place
5 = complete

Table 4.1 Process Development Checklist

	1	2	3	4	5	Company Priority	Comments
Corporate Ethics							
Code of Conduct							
Planning							
Strategic/Business Plan							
Marketing Plan							
Operations Plans							
Budget preparation							
Performance metrics							
Finance/Accounting							
Periodic reports							
A/R & Collections							
Inventory							
A/P							
Cash management							
Expense management							
Revenue assurance							
Audits							
Legal/Regulatory							
Compliance							
Reporting							
Sales							
Forecasts							
Results reporting							
Discount policies							
Marketing							
Pricing guidelines							
Product development							
Channel management							
Operations							
Purchasing							
Production/fulfillment							
Quality assurance							
Returns							
Maintenance/repairs							

Table 4.1 (*Continued*)

	1	2	3	4	5	Company Priority	Comments
Customer Service							
Customer change requests							
Customer repair & maintenance							
Complaint handling							
Escalation procedures							
Returns and adjustments							
MIS/IT							
Disaster recovery							
Project identification & prioritization							
Project management							
HW/SW testing and deployment							
Help desk							
Human Resources							
Recruiting/screening							
Orientation/training							
Job descriptions							
Compliance							
Reporting							
Salary administration							
Succession planning							
Employee handbook							
Employee communications							
Performance management							
Facility Management							

Process and Bureaucracy

Our inability to provide guidance that insures that processes never evolve into stifling bureaucracy now becomes evident. A growing company's ability to implement sound processes but not veer into unnecessary bureaucracy is dependent on many variables:

- The industry and associated compliance requirements.
- The complexity of the company's product or service and the needs of its customers.
- The pace of growth.

- The backgrounds, experiences, and management styles of the senior and middle management team.
- The company's ability to focus on its core competencies and strategies.
- The capital available.
- The company's ability to not allow itself to incur expenses incumbent with unnecessary bureaucracy.

All of these factors and others churn incessantly as the company grows, but ultimately the presence or absence of bureaucracy boils down to a matter of the management team's ability and will to walk a thin tightrope—falling off one side fuels chaos; falling off the other creates a burdensome drag a growth company cannot afford.

DSII-MORDE

Every day executives make decisions, both major and minor. The decisions must support the company's strategies (assuming the strategies are valid) and often involve determining priorities, for capital, resources, time, attention, and the like.

All too often executives make decisions in a stressful environment that has too many distractions. This leads to poor choices being made and opportunities missed. This is not due to management incompetence, but because of the intense and volatile environment that is the defining characteristic of high-growth companies.

As an example, a company with a nonunion workforce was rapidly building and acquiring additional facilities. After one such acquisition the company learned that the employees at the new facility were represented by a collective bargaining agreement, with the Teamsters. Talk about the right hand not knowing what the left hand . . .

Are tools and approaches available that can make executives more effective in their administration of day-to-day business? We believe so, and they aren't rocket science or earth-shaking. They utilize tried and proven methodologies, just with a new spin.

Every business book author must invent an acronym or two. Here's one of ours:

DSII-MORDE.

In our sixty-five-plus years in business we have observed a phenomenon with alarming regularity: decisions being made (or not made) utilizing one or more of the following approaches:

- *Pure Intuition:* The "I'm smart as hell and have all the moving pieces identified in my head" approach. This may work for geniuses and in small operations, but is unlikely to deliver consistently high-quality decisions.
- *Conventional Wisdom:* The "This issue has come up before and I know how we dealt with it then, so we'll do the same thing now" approach. Perhaps this is reasonable in environments that never experience change.
- *Committee:* The "Let's get some people together to talk about it" approach. This is not invalid in and of itself, but often the "committee" gets sidetracked and will insert too much irrelevant data or functional partisanship.
- *Divine Intervention:* The "Lets sleep on it and discuss it tomorrow" approach. Somehow "tomorrow" never comes, and the issue doesn't go away but returns with a vengeance.
- *Analysis:* The "Lets crunch the numbers" approach. This is valid in context, but can overlook variables other than "the numbers."
- *Political:* The "How will this look?" approach. Enough said.

Some of these approaches, or at least certain attributes of them, are logical and reasonable. Others, by themselves, may look at only some of the variables. The optimum approach synthesizes the best qualities of all, becomes intuitive, and yields the highest-quality results.

The DSII-MORDE "Non–Rocket Science" Approach

"Return on one thing or another" Return on Investment (ROI), Return on Equity (ROE) analyses are familiar to readers, and we will not bore you with an explanation here . . . except to say, the basic concept of getting answers to the what, why, and how much questions intrinsic to return analyses are core components of *DSII-MORDE.* Though not as quantitative, *DSII-MORDE* shares a core characteristic of ROI analysis: orderly thinking.

DSII-MORDE: The agenda for decision-making:

- Clearly and specifically **Define** the decision that must be made. Write it down.
- Determine if the decision is substantively relevant to the environment in which the company operates, its competencies, and its **Strategies**. Check the "wallet card" . . . more on that later.
- Define the **Implications** of the decision. What are the results if the right decision is made? The wrong one?

- Define any additional *Information* required to make a decision.
- Define the *Magnitude* of the decision—revenue/costs; resources required; time required; "mindshare" required.
- Define the existing and potential *Options*.
- Define the *"Return"* of all the options.
- Identify the best option and *Decide*.
- *Execute*.

DSII-MORDE is, admittedly, a reconstituted dose of common sense. This simple process that, if followed, improves the quality and timeliness of decision-making in the frantic world of high-growth companies.

The "Wallet Card," Figuratively Speaking

Everyday decision-making must be considered part of the planning process; therefore, it is a process, not a daily series of knee-jerk reactions. The decision-making process is a "mini" version of what occurs in formal planning sessions.

Management must utilize and demand that others use the *DSII-MORDE* model. Every employee must anticipate that management will conduct meetings by following the process. Thus, they will prepare accordingly...and better decisions will be the result.

So, as senior managers, pull out the mental "wallet card" that lists the decision-making steps. Follow the steps and soon all your subordinates will. An orderly decision-making process will begin to permeate the organization, and soon the structure of good planning will become integrated into everyday execution.

MOVING THE MONKEY

Well over thirty years ago, when Rodney was a lowly sales representative, my district manager came in one morning carrying a stuffed monkey. Though he was prone to unusual behaviors, this was beyond the norm. I inquired about the monkey (no one else had the courage or lack of judgment to do so), and he asked me to his office and discussed a seminar he had just completed. To summarize, the seminar's topic was the art of delegation, and the particular gimmick was "moving the monkey" of responsibility from the manager to subordinates. The story stuck with me all these years and has relevance to the senior management of growth companies.

The Early Days

The founding management team, by necessity, was made up of both doers and managers. Depending on when the executives joined the company, they may have been mostly doers. The scenario is familiar; everyone did a little of everything; everyone was a salesperson; everyone took customer calls. In short, no matter their professional backgrounds, the senior management of the company got its "hands dirty" every day.

Even during early growth, a few supervisors and managers were hired, but management was only one level removed from task work. They possessed the subject matter expertise on all issues and often found it easier to complete a task than teach someone else how to do it. This situation changed over time as the company began to grow; some executives easily evolved to management and, later, executive roles. Others found it more difficult.

Self-Evaluation

The senior management teams of high-growth companies should earnestly evaluate their delegation skills on a periodic basis. Perhaps more than any other facet of their job, the evolving requirements of delegation are the most dynamic. As company and departmental functions grow and mature, what gets delegated and to whom changes with every reorganization, every major hiring decision, and every change in responsibilities and assignments. All of these occurrences are ceaseless in a growth company.

The objective here is not to develop a delegation tutorial. But there are several basic suggestions that should help you assess your delegation effectiveness:

- Don't accept a problem without demanding recommendations for a solution. You should require your subordinates to bring 1) well-defined problems with associated implications, and 2) well-thought-out potential solutions, each with their pros and cons. Insist that they do most of the *DSII-MORDE* work. Don't take the monkey.
- Don't instinctively take on the problem and try to fix it. You may know more about the issue than anyone, but investing the time to coach

your subordinates so they can solve the problem next time is well worth it. Remember the old fable about the effectiveness of teaching someone how to fish rather than giving them a fish.

• Realize if you take the "monkey" too often, you are unconsciously sending two messages. You're convincing yourself you have no confidence in your subordinates. And, you're convincing subordinates that you have no confidence in them. If this behavior continues it will spiral down to a point you will eventually blast the employees, perhaps fire them, and they will not have the slightest idea why.

Additionally, it is recommended that as a part of the "quarterly time-outs" each senior manager compares her responsibilities and current organization with what it was the previous quarter. Each executive should discuss those changes and, as a group, share thoughts on how each may alter how they manage their organizations. This exercise provides an opportunity for much-needed introspection. Additionally, other team members can benefit from learning how each department's decision-making process may be changing.

Importance

One may wonder why a section has been devoted to such a seemingly mundane issue: delegation. We hope the answer is obvious. A growth company presents its senior managers with constantly increasing and changing responsibilities. Those responsibilities are more complex and demanding than those that existed six months before. To deal with this, executives must learn how to get the most out of their subordinates. "Doing" is no longer an option. Just surrounding themselves with capable lieutenants will not get the job done, either.

Hiring high-quality people is the first step. Using them effectively is the mandatory second step.

"We Don't Have Time"

Of course you don't! There's never enough time to do what needs to be done in a high-growth company. The shifting and growing demands of management's time are overwhelming, and the long hours worked in the start-up pale in comparison. Not only is more time required, the stakes are higher. You may have been up to midnight sealing envelopes and licking stamps to get the invoices out on time earlier; now you're dealing with more weighty matters: overseeing a systems cutover, traveling back from a meeting of potential investors, or struggling to get a new product out on time.

Whatever the reasons, let's face it, there just isn't enough time. This chapter acknowledges that but looks at what senior managers can do to not make things worse. It's almost impossible to do what needs to be done if everybody is working as efficiently as possible. It is impossible if they are not.

Causes of Self-Inflicted Inefficiency

Growth companies and their senior management teams do not have the luxury of wasting time, yet the very nature of a high-growth environment sows the seeds for inefficiency. The reasons were identified earlier: constant changes in the environment and the company, growth in sales volume, new employees, and employees having to do things differently than how they were done just three months earlier. The luxury of stability that slow/no-growth companies and huge corporations enjoy is no more than a fantasy. But somehow amidst the turmoil, you must cope and not make it worse. We think the term is "not shooting yourself in the foot."

Therefore, the challenge is to first understand what leads to the waste of precious time. The reasons fall into three broad categories:

- Lack of clear priorities
- General corporate disorganization
- Personal disorganization

Lack of Clear Priorities The company's priorities originate in the plan that is approved by the board and communicated to the organization by senior management. This process should lead to universal and unequivocal understanding by everyone as to what's really important. However, the dynamic environment in which growth companies exist constantly presents distractions, starts "fires" that must be extinguished, and brings to light issues that necessitate alterations of course. But, barring catastrophes, rarely do they change the company's core priorities.

Yet time and time again in dealing with the "issue du jour," senior teams allow their focus to wander, or create the perception that it's wandering. Employees have the remarkable ability to sense what their bosses think is important. And, subordinates will concentrate on what their boss says is important. Therefore, with words, deeds, body language, or memos, an executive can inadvertently reorder the business's priorities in the minds of employees.

Senior managers do not intend to send confusing messages. Ideally, they fully comprehend the company's priorities and the broader context of an insinuation or specific tactical guidance...but their employees may not. If that's the case, the employees trudge off muttering such things as "I wonder how long this will be the number one priority" or "Who the hell's on first?"

These observations do not ignore the daily requirement of adjusting priorities to deal with the inevitable surprises. However, they do appeal to the senior managers' need to understand the importance of perception management. When middle management *thinks* it is going off in a hundred different directions with no guidance, it really is. When they *think* they are working on projects that are conflicting and fragmenting their efforts, they are. And, when they *think* senior management is not focused, it isn't.

If middle management and the rest of the employees do not clearly understand the company's priorities and/or believe they are working toward conflicting objectives, the negative impact on the company's efficiency is startling. Some people simply shut down, incapable of producing meaningful work. Some demonstrate their frustration by discussing the situation with others, and the corporate grapevine goes into overdrive. Some may leave the company, convinced that senior management hasn't a clue as to what direction the company should take.

Consider a medium-size service company. Senior management had done a good job of explaining the strategic direction of the company. It was a tough industry, however, and a down cycle began industrywide. Everyone began to notice the officers constantly behind closed doors and in lots of meeting. Trust us, the troops don't miss much.

As you might imagine, the rumor mill started and résumés were being updated. The truth was that the company actually had a good plan after a few adjustments, and everything was okay. Not until the misperceptions were corrected could everyone go about doing their jobs.

Whatever the reaction of employees, the consequences of such miscommunication are confusion, misunderstanding, a lack of focus, and conflicting priorities, and they simply kill productivity. Time is wasted and quality of work suffers, just at the time the company can least afford it.

General Corporate Disorganization Companies, like human beings, have their own personalities and ways of doing things. It's generally called corporate culture, and we will address that topic in more detail later, but the concept is germane to the subject at hand.

As with many issues discussed in this book, the impact of the founding senior management team is significant in the development of the "personality" of the company. The company's overall planning and organizing capabilities are a prime example.

If basic orderliness and a structured pattern to doing business were present at the beginning, it is likely the company evolved with those traits. Process development was a natural and relatively easy undertaking. The added formality with which business must be conducted in a larger company developed almost intuitively. And, fundamental practices of communications, planning, meeting effectiveness, and the like became normal ways of conducting business.

However, if the corporate environment during start-up was erratic, without structure, and informal, it is probable that those characteristics remain even though the company is much larger. Fundamental organizing and planning skills may be absent or not used effectively. The lack of solid strategic/tactical planning, intrateam communications, and structured meeting formats all contribute to disorganization. And disorganization reduces efficiency, leads to duplicated efforts, and sets a kind of "cowboy" tone for the company that is not conducive to the disciplines required to sustain growth.

Characteristics of disorganization; the meaningful and the mundane:

- Promised reports or updates are delivered late, and the provider and recipient aren't upset or surprised.
- Meetings hardly ever start on time; there's never an agenda.
- Senior managers have no idea what other managers are doing.
- Senior and middle managers are out of the office; no one know where they are.
- The employee newsletter is always late, and overlooks someone's birthday.
- Financials are late getting to the board.
- Systems upgrades are made before anyone is trained on how to use them.
- Customer complaints get lost in the shuffle and no one ever solves the problem.
- W-2s are sent out late.
- The website has outdated information . . . from eighteen months ago.
- Sales initiates a discount program and nobody told customer service.

Disorganization's bedfellows are poor processes and poor communications. But the example senior management sets creates the aura that will facilitate the company in getting its act together.

Personal Disorganization No, you're not going to be subjected to a time management lecture. But you will be asked to conduct a personal assessment of work habits that might have an impact on your individual productivity... and how your work habits might be interpreted by your employees.

Similar to the self-analysis discussed in the previous chapter, senior managers in growth companies are compelled to analyze their work habits in a changing environment. What may have been very effective twelve months ago may no longer be. And, what works now may need adjustment next year.

The assumption again is that the rules are constantly changing. Adaptation and individual growth are necessary. We all are naturally equipped with a certain management style and work habits. They form the foundation of how we go about doing business every day. But that doesn't mean they cannot be improved or altered as the requirements of the job change. That is particularly true as it relates to how you use your time, and your use of time effects how others use theirs.

Senior managers in growth companies should view their time similarly to consultants and attorneys in terms of looking at activities and productivity on an hourly basis. Competent and ethical professionals who bill their services by the hour are ever conscious of the value they are delivering to the client. They realize their clients will and should evaluate the benefits received from one unit of work, typically an hour. That evaluation creates an inner tension and motivation to deliver and meet the clients' expectations.

Senior executives' time is no less valuable and expensive to the company than that of the professionals it engages... in many cases it is more so. Therefore, the attitudinal yardstick that should determine how senior managers use their time is:

"Am I doing those things that are most critical to the company and am I doing them in the most efficient way possible in order to maximize my contribution to the company?"

While we're at it... Should this question be asked by every employee in the organization? And, if yes, what sorts of examples, good and bad, are set by the senior team?

Company/Individual Efficiency Assessment

The following self-assessment provides a quick look at the three factors that impact efficiency in the company. An honest and thoughtful rating of your degree of agreement with the statements will provide insight into how you and your team can make the most of the fourteen-hour days growth companies require.

Indicate your agreement/disagreement with the following statements:
1. Totally disagree
2. Somewhat disagree
3. Don't know
4. Somewhat agree
5. Totally agree

Table 4.2 Company/Individual Efficiency Assessment

Company Priorities	1	2	3	4	5
The company's strategy imperatives are understood and agreed to by all.					
Senior and middle management can clearly articulate the company's major strategies and top five priorities at the moment . . . from memory.					
The management team will agree that the company is focused and working on the right things.					
The management team will agree that there is consistency in the company's focus.					
The entire organization believes that senior management is completely aligned in its interpretations of the company's highest priorities.					
Company's General Organizational Competencies					
The company has the most critical processes in place and they are working.					
The management team has regular meetings with formal agendas.					
Meetings start and end on time.					
All the employees meet the commitments they make in terms of timeliness.					
Everyone in the company is completely clear on their duties and responsibilities.					
Employees are equipped to effectively handle most of the issues they deal with daily.					

Table 4.2 (*Continued*)

Company Priorities	1	2	3	4	5
Individual Organizational Competencies					
75% of the day is planned before it begins.					
50% of the next week is planned.					
You have agendas prepared for all your formal meetings.					
You make constant use of a daily planner...paper or electronic.					
You return all phone calls and e-mails within twenty-four hours.					

Learning from Screwups

Much has been written about growth and innovation environments, specifically citing a company's ability to "accept failure" as a major supportive characteristic. The aggressive product deployment strategies of 3M, Nike, and Polo have produced more than their share of failures, but these companies understand that a high-growth strategy will produce failures, and they learn from them and move on.

The inference, of course, is that experimentation and original thinking are stimulated if the company's environment does not overtly punish those who have ideas that don't quite work out. A reasonable approach no doubt, but it must be applied with moderation and exceptionally good judgment in high-growth companies.

What We Can Learn from the Scientists

The scientific disciplines utilize a testing and verification protocol that has applications in growth companies. In a layman's view, they use a nonemotional, fact-based process to determine if a given theory, formula, or supposition is valid. If the desired outcome does not transpire, they carefully analyze what they did—step-by-step—and attempt to identify the source of the problem. They make the correction and move on. There are no negative repercussions; the scientists are completely focused on fixing what went wrong.

This method of addressing screwups delivers tangible benefits to your company.

The Process

Following are the recommended steps for what we call a "Project Debriefing." Note the lack of a negative connotation. Even though focusing on projects that had less than positive outcomes, the process is equally effective in determining what went right and identifying actions that you want to replicate in the future.

PROJECT DEBRIEFING STEPS

Planning Review

- What were the original objectives?
- What were the planning assumptions?
- What options were identified?
- Were the appropriate resources made available?
- Was the plan fundamentally sound?

Execution Review

- Were the steps in execution logical?
- Were the steps of execution sequenced properly?
- Who was involved in the execution?
- What external factors/resources were involved in execution?
- What was the quality of execution?

Analysis

- Were the original assumptions correct?
- What went right/wrong?
- Why?
- What could have been done to alter/improve the outcome?
- What are the lessons learned?
- How will the lessons be applied to future projects?

We don't know that Andy Grove of Intel used our model (likely not), but his company's success can, in part, be attributed to his leadership style and skills in gaining full understanding of why some projects were successful and others not.

Requisites for Successful Debriefings

Not to get hung up on semantics, but growth companies, frankly, cannot tolerate too much failure, but they can create an environment where the company learns from its mistakes.

Thankfully, most growth companies have not yet acquired the static, slothlike, and political characteristics of larger established companies. More common is a pervasive "can-do" and "let's get on with it" work environment. With that sort of attitude, much can and should be learned from past mistakes.

For the Project Debriefing approach to be most productive, the management team must insure that the exercise is void of any obvious or covert actions or attitudes motivated by anything other than just trying to learn and get better. Following are the desired characteristics of the process in order for Project Debriefing to produce the desired results:

- Minimize "winners" and "losers," individuals and departments; the only winner or loser is the company. If it learns to do things better, it is a winner; if it doesn't, the effort was a waste of time.
- Beware of the "blame game"; if something went amiss, the process will identify it in short order. There is no need for finger-pointing.
- It's not a "witch hunt"; the company does not hire witches, so there are none to be found.
- No "feeding frenzy"; if one begins, the sharks are probably a bigger problem than the bait.
- There are no "career-killers"; the company has gracious few talented people; it has no interest in punishing those who are extending themselves to get things done.

GE (there's little dispute regarding its success) calls its process "the Workout." It's employed at the conclusion of any project that did not meet stringent expectations.

- Organize a nonmanagerial, cross-functional project team.
- Provide its members the data to allow them to understand the project's objectives, its development history, and its outcome/results.
- Charge them with analyzing the project and identifying enhancements to similar future projects.
- Have them report their recommendations to a responsible senior manager who has to approve or reject (with justification) each recommendation *on the spot.*

Whether you conduct GE's "Workouts" or follow our suggested regimen, we cannot emphasize enough the value of learning from history. It teaches a lot to all of us.

Chapter 5

MAXIMIZING LEADERSHIP
EFFECTIVENESS

THE MORAL COMPASSES

The previous four chapters addressed many of the "hard" elements of managing a successful growth company: planning, process development, budgeting, and more. Though we intentionally sought to minimize the "soft" factors, a review of the previous chapters clearly shows that we were not totally successful. Human nature proved impossible to eliminate from even the most analytical process.

That said, the intent of this chapter is to directly address the "softer" factors required for a growth company's success. Ethics, leadership, and corporate culture all have a tremendous impact on the company, most directly on the people. Without a solid and supportive moral underpinning, a company's growth is not sustainable.

Note the Plural: Compasses

This book has so far been directed to the entire senior management team, especially in its capacity to set the agendas and serve as an example for all the people in middle management and on the front line. Everyone shares responsibility for the company's planning and execution. They also share responsibility for defining the ethics of the company. The team's leader has unique responsibilities, to be discussed later, but the executive team as a whole should not abdicate its social obligations to the company and its employees.

Do the Right Thing

Simple guidance, simple to communicate, but with powerful ramifications.

This simple directive makes a basic assumption: The team knows what the right thing is. This is not a morals lesson, but you know the right thing to do if:

- The team is trustworthy.
- The team is fair.
- The team is consistent.
- The team tells the truth.

Those qualities provide the moral foundation to do the right thing...and the right thing doesn't mean just not doing the wrong thing. As members of the senior management team, you have the ability to make decisions that insure that others do nothing wrong and, if they do, to correct it.

Perception Is Reality

Someone said the road to hell is paved with good intentions. Said another way, no matter the senior team's moral strength and integrity, if the employees perceive something different, it is different. How would your employees answer the following questions?

- What five adjectives would best describe the management team?
- What behaviors does the senior management team reward?
- In a crisis, does the management team behave differently?
- Who gets promoted in the company and why?
- Who "fits" in the company and who doesn't?
- Does the management team keep its word?
- Do you trust them?

A positive perception of the management team is mandatory. Creating a positive tone for the company requires winning the minds and hearts of the employees. Competence wins the minds. Trust wins the hearts.

A breakdown in competence can be remedied. Everyone screws up sometimes, and the employees realize that. A breakdown in trust is rarely overcome. When the employees trust their leadership, they are capable of remarkable performance. The very same group with the very same skills and knowledge will not respond to leadership they don't trust.

The margin for error on the trust issue is very slim. A moment of inconsistency, a promotion that is not well researched, a "white lie" that spirals out of control...all negatively influence the employees' perception of the trustworthiness of the management team.

Ethics Aren't Situational

Ethical behavior is doing the right thing when nobody's looking. Expediency and job pressures sometimes test every management team, but sticking to the core ethics will, when it's all said and done, serve the company well.

The following fictional vignettes could test a management team's ethical resolve. How would your team react?

The company has developed its ethics code and corporate values and spent considerable efforts in communicating them to the employee body. One of its top sales producers, long known to operate "on the edge," does so once again and the transgression is brought to the attention of senior management. The salesperson is working on a huge opportunity that means a lot to the company, and terminating him will jeopardize the deal.

A well-respected middle manager is discovered to have a business on the side. She's extremely competent, perhaps destined for senior management one day. Her business activities do not present a clear conflict of interest, but they're in direct violation of the company's code of conduct...which she signed.

A generally amiable senior executive had a few too many beers at a company social function and berated a middle manager for real and imaginary performance problems in front of the manager's peers. Apparently the executive had problems with this middle manager for years but never opened his mouth until this outburst.

A customer service representative advises HR that his supervisor is engaging in fraudulent activity. Investigation confirms the accusation. Independent of the fraud situation, the supervisor turns in the rep's performance review for approval and is recommending termination. The case is sound. The rep's performance is deplorable and he's been given every opportunity to improve.

A senior team member proposes a major promotion in her department. She has prepared a sterling case. The individual has been rated highly for two years. He has excelled at everything he's done, according to his boss. The other team members have never dealt with the individual to any great degree, but those few interactions had been painful. He is the biggest "brown-noser" in the company.

After an intense negotiating session with a supplier, an employee discovers some papers the supplier's representative accidentally left behind in the conference room. The information would give the company a significant negotiating advantage if they were not returned to the supplier.

The media has picked up some erroneous information about a new product. If it were true, it would have a major positive impact in the marketplace, but it's not. There's really no downside to providing a "no comment" to the reporter...except it's clear she will publish the story unless it's specifically denied.

Think about it.

LEADERSHIP AND MOTIVATION

What can be written that hasn't already been written? Not a lot, but we will offer a couple of perspectives that have particular relevance to the senior management team.

What Is Leadership?

In a business environment, we define leadership as the ability of *senior management* to provide an *environment* of *mutual trust* that encourages employees to conduct the company's business with *high quality* and to do so *willingly*.

Senior Management: It's the responsibility of the whole management team.
Environment: It encompasses everything the management team says and does.
Mutual trust: Nobody leads or follows effectively if they are constantly looking over their shoulder.
High quality: Mediocrity is achievable without good leadership.
Willingly: The employees must want to do a good job to do a good job.

All Politics Is Local, So Is Leadership

The team's natural leadership skills were exhibited easily when the company was small. There were few if any subleaders; the executives led by example, and their leadership was up close and personal. They touched everything and everybody every day. Of course, things changed.

Management practices change as the company grows; so do leadership practices in a similar way. Many years ago we developed a supposition that has been validated in the years since: Employees put the most emphasis on what their immediate supervisors say is important; therefore, supervisors and managers up and down the line have a more direct impact on the employee base than the executives.

The implication is that senior management must not only lead personally, it must learn to lead through others. As the company grows, its leadership must make its way through several management layers to get to the people who do the real work—selling the product, making the product, fulfilling the service, supporting customers. Only those who report directly to senior management experience its leadership qualities firsthand.

Sure, there are occasions when the officers address a large meeting or meet with smaller groups of employees, but leadership must be strong and clear enough to not be diluted as the company grows. Time must be taken to insure that managers and supervisors completely understand what is expected. As a member of senior management, you must make the time to talk to them and reinforce their belief in you.

What Do the Followers Expect?

In order to deliver effective leadership, the team must understand the expectations of the followers. Research over the years indicates a consistent pattern of priorities in terms of what motivates employees, thus guiding senior managers on how they should lead. Surprisingly perhaps, the most important motivators relate more to leadership than remuneration. In order of priority they are:

- Awareness and appreciation of their efforts
- Being informed about the company; where it is, where its going, how it's doing
- Sensitivity to their personal situations and getting support when needed
- Job security
- Challenging and meaningful work assignments

- Compensation and benefits
- The company's loyalty to the employees
- Opportunity for growth
- A positive work environment

The majority of these motivators are closely related to the team's leadership styles and communications.

Team and Individual Leadership Assessment

The desirable attributes of leaders are intuitive, but it never hurts to take a few introspective minutes and assess your team and yourself. Be honest in the self-evaluation and give particular thought to identifying examples where a particular leadership trait has been exhibited (or not exhibited) by you or the team.

LEADERSHIP SELF-ASSESSMENT

5 = Continually exhibited
4 = Exhibited quite often
3 = Exhibited occasionally
2 = Not exhibited often
1 = Exhibited seldom if ever

Table 5.1 Leadership Self-Assessment

Leadership Trait	5	4	3	2	1	Examples
Honesty, integrity, and forthrightness						
The team						
ME						
Balances idealism and realism						
The team						
ME						
Completely understands the company's growth vision and communicates it effectively						
The team						
ME						

Table 5.1 (*Continued*)

Leadership Trait	5	4	3	2	1	Examples
Will listen						
The team						
ME						
Totally committed to the success of the company as whole						
The team						
ME						
Competence						
The team						
ME						
Confidence, not arrogance						
The team						
ME						
Genuine care for the employees						
The team						
ME						
Communicates openly and honestly						
The team						
ME						
Hard work						
The team						
ME						
Is motivated						
The team						
ME						
Leads by example						
The team						
ME						
Provides clear direction						
The team						
ME						
Delegates; doesn't oversupervise						
The team						
ME						

Table 5.1 (*Continued*)

Leadership Trait	5	4	3	2	1	Examples
Steady during crisis						
The team						
ME						
Stimulates the heart and mind						
The team						
ME						
Builds self-esteem in others						
The team						
ME						
Develops others						
The team						
ME						

UNIQUE CHALLENGES FOR THE "BOSS"

This book places intentional emphasis on the senior management team as a whole. With rare exception, growth companies seldom succeed solely on the wit, wisdom, and individual leadership of the CEO, COO, president, chairman, whatever the title is of the person who really runs things. Assembling a talented senior management team and working with and through them is absolutely critical. One individual may be able to unilaterally run a small or no-growth company, but the challenges of growth require the collective skills, knowledge, and leadership strengths of a strong team, and the willingness and ability of the boss to use them effectively.

That said, every successful team obviously requires a boss: the leader, the deciding vote, the arbiter, the individual where the buck ultimately stops. Collaborative decision-making has its limitations. Someone must make the final decisions about difficult and hugely important issues. Someone must answer to the board. That's the boss, and these are terribly critical and unique responsibilities the other team members do not have.

Expanding and Evolving Requirements

The mandatory changes required of growth companies have been addressed in many contexts. However, few are as dramatic and important as those that the boss must experience. Everyone else's job descriptions may evolve over time, but the boss's must be completely rewritten several times as the company grows in both size and complexity.

Bosses must not only master new skills, they must be clever enough to identify them ahead of time, to perceive where the company is going and forecast what they will need to know and do six months or a year from now. They must not only do this for themselves, but also for their senior team.

Over the course of several years, the leader's evolution goes through several phases, generally aligned with the stages of the company's growth.

Entrepreneurial In the beginning the boss is a doer and decision-maker. Intimate knowledge of the industry and market is essential. So too are cash management, supplier negotiations, customer contacts, and everything else, including the kitchen sink. Some of these responsibilities are transferred to others as the senior team begins to take shape. Obtaining customers is paramount. However, the leadership required to keep the company afloat is and will remain the boss's personal responsibility.

Early Growth Spurt The company is increasing in mass and complexity, and the boss removes himself from many of the day-to-day activities. The management team is coalescing, and organizational development and delegation become priorities. Vice presidents, managers and supervisors begin to fill slots. The boss becomes intimately involved in activities to fund the company, seeking sources of capital to finance the ever-expanding enterprise. Determining the direction of the company and formalizing its planning processes become priorities. The headaches of growth also dominate, and the boss and team must pay increasing attention to infrastructure and process development. Leadership is required to keep the wheels from falling off and to fund the results of the company's success.

Adolescence The management team is in place and the organizational structure is basically sound. Assistant vice presidents, directors, and more managers are in place. The boss remains focused on funding the company, but efforts are now at a whole new level of sophistication. Planning likewise must mature to satisfy the requirements of lenders and investors. Departments form, and insuring cooperation and coordinated unity of purpose requires increasing attention in order to avoid crippling bureaucracy. Building and overseeing teams is critical and time-consuming. The boss's leadership in the past kept the wheels on, now it must stimulate them to roll faster and faster.

Maturity The management team likely requires change, always a leader-ship challenge. Acquisitions and an IPO become viable and require considerable attention. The boss must, more than ever before, think "outside the box" and become a strategic innovator, not just within the company but the industry. He needs to be seen and heard outside the confines of the company. Leadership is what takes the company to the "promised land."

Coping

Though these summaries are far from complete, one senses the magnitude of the breadth and depth of the competencies and leadership qualities the boss must master. Precious few individuals are blessed with the "total package." We know of none.

The boss's ability and desire to catalog his strengths and weaknesses and identify the "gaps" at different stages of the company's growth are necessary exercises in self-development. Then, filling the "gaps" becomes the priority.

The Senior Team Building a team that possesses complementary competencies and leadership skills is the most obvious and important tool available to the boss. Team members can and should bring talents to the company that go beyond any particular functional competencies. They should bring networking capabilities that offer value to both the company as a whole and the boss specifically. They should bring complementary communications skills. A broad array of formal educational backgrounds is helpful. Most of all, they should bring a spirit of cooperation and support. Bosses, whether they realize it or not, need all the help they can get.

The Board The board of directors should provide meaningful advice and counsel to the boss. It is likely the board is composed of individuals who are successful in their own realms. Their success may have come in different industries or professions, but the aggregate business acumen and experience is immense. The board members should be intensely interested in the boss's success because it's directly linked to that of the company. In recent years board activism has been presented in the context of oversight of corporate misbehavior. However, such activism can manifest itself in very positive and meaningful ways, specifically in supporting and counseling roles for the boss. Bosses should not allow their egos to negate the positive influence of this vast repository of potential assistance.

Support Groups No, this doesn't suggest that bosses need some sort of addiction or mental health counseling. Numerous ad hoc CEO groups exists, many of them composed of leaders of growth companies. Though in different industries, growth companies share many common challenges and problems. Dialogue among a group with similar concerns is restorative and a source for good ideas. Additionally, many industry trade associations have "CEO forums" where members of like companies can address common issues.

Chief Executive Network: http://www.chiefexec.com/
Senior Executive Network: http://www.chiefexec.com/aboutSEN.htm

Executive Education Many universities offer courses and seminars that address the challenges executives face in high-growth companies as well as general development education. The following websites are a small sample of programs available.

- Leading Strategic Growth and Change; Columbia Business School, Columbia University; http://www.gsb.columbia.edu/execed/open/programs/lsgc.cfm
- Finding Profitable Growth Strategies; School of Business, University of Wisconsin-Madison; http://www.uwexeced.com/advancedmanagement/growth.htm
- Strategies for Emerging and Rapidly Growing Businesses (web based); Jones International University; http://www.jonesinternational.edu/ourPrograms/course.php?crs=157
- Building and Implementing Growth Strategies; Graduate School of Business, University of Chicago; http://www.chicagoexec.net/chicago.nsf/PROGRAM?openview&id=37
- Executive Program for Growing Companies; Graduate School of Business, Stanford University; http://www.gsb.stanford.edu/exed/epgc/
- Strategic Finance for Smaller Businesses; Harvard Business School, Harvard University; http://www.exed.hbs.edu/programs/sfsb/

Executive Coaching Jack Welch used one, so it shouldn't be deflating to the ego. Seriously, many competent consultants specialize in working with growth companies and their senior executives. Bosses sometimes have issues that are confidential and sensitive, and an external sounding board can sometimes make all the difference.

The emotional and intellection demands of the boss of a growth company are almost unfathomable. Skills that were relevant yesterday aren't today. The company must be run daily, yet time must be found to make accurate prognostications about what's going to be happening a year from now. Sometimes there's simply no one to talk to. The list is endless.

Yet, somehow, the boss must deal with it all, successfully and gracefully. Leading a growth company is one of the toughest yet most rewarding jobs that exists.

CULTURE: SO IMPORTANT

This book discussed many topics, some "hard," some "soft." But no issue is more amorphous than that of corporate culture. It's everywhere, but you can't put your hands on it. It impacts everything, but it's difficult to develop a "culture strategy." It can make or break a growth company.

Culture: What Is It?

A slightly modified dictionary definition: *"The shared values, beliefs, customs, practices and social behaviors of a company."*

The definition is very broad and intentionally so. Culture is founded in the history and folklore of the company. It has an impact on the company's organizational structure. It impacts job descriptions and compensation. It influences the company's performance management system. It defines the collective expectations of the company. It impacts the responsibility-accountability continuum. And, it subtlety determines how ambitious the company's growth vision can be and whether or not its strategies can be effectively implemented.

That's because the culture is pervasive, influencing all levels of the company's activities. On the surface it is reflected in the company's social structure, the company's employee functions, what's on the employees' desks, the dress code.

It's also reflected in company practices and processes, its employment practices, finding and hiring the kind of people the company wants. The concept of teamwork and whether or not it's really practiced is dependent on the culture.

And, at its deepest, it's inexorably linked to the company's ethics and the leadership practices of the executives.

Were the Good Old Days Really Good?

This book has addressed the "good old days" throughout, generally to emphasize the dramatic change that growth companies experience. And, an implication is probably obvious to the reader...the old days were good; life was simpler; everyone knew each other; it was a family. It was a great culture...or was it really?

Before looking at the growth culture, it is instructive to look back dispassionately at an earlier culture. It may be remembered fondly, but should a growth company attempt to try to replicate it, even if it could?

It seemed great to operate in an unstructured environment...few rules, "winging it," no encumbrances to get in the way of really serving the customers.

But, how well were the customers served when the company had few if any quality standards?

There weren't any purchasing guidelines; we worked closely and personally with our suppliers and just worked things out without a whole lot of hassle.

But, how much more did the company pay when it was a high credit risk and did not possess keen negotiating capabilities?

Intuitively determining pricing and discounts, being able to "do a deal" on the fly without having to get approval from anyone was wonderful.

But, how much lost profit and opportunity resulted in the freewheeling discounting?

Finances were tight and it was a struggle to meet payroll some weeks. But the company persevered, got through it, and is proud it did. As well it should be.

But, how effective was management when it was constantly focused on simply surviving?

The company gave raises when people really deserved them. People knew they would be rewarded if they worked hard, and there wasn't all this paperwork and formality.

But, with no oversight, what disparities in compensation were created. In addition to disharmony (we're convinced that everyone in a company knows what everyone else makes), did the company inadvertently create legal exposure?

For growth companies, the "old days" are rapidly becoming ancient history. As the scenarios show, those days probably weren't that great anyway. Those days will never return. Get on with the new culture.

Anti-Growth Cultures

A healthy growth culture begins by understanding cultural characteristics to avoid. Below are four stereotypical cultures that have characteristics that may be in evidence in your company.

The Bunker A retreat for the fearful and indecisive. Everything is viewed as the ultimate risk. The glass of water is always half-empty. Prudence dissolves into paralysis. For any number of reasons, employees are afraid to make decisions. It could be leadership that concentrates all decision-making at the very top, second-guessing and criticizing everyone and everything. The leaders take credit for good decisions others make and abdicate any responsibility for decisions that go awry. A question everyone asks themselves: "Why make a decision?"

The Fraternity A clique runs the company...a clique not necessarily limited to members of senior management. There's an unstated requirement for conformity, and any deviation will insure that an individual won't join the clique. Informal power bases bypass the normal decision-making process. Outsiders up and down the organization know they are outsiders. And, the fraternity has the power to throw out existing members as well as "blackball" new pledges.

Lets Just All Get Along The culture simply cannot deal with opposing points of view and honest disagreement, much less conflict. Formal decision-making breaks down and things get done by anyone who puts together a few supporters and just starts doing them. The actions may or may not be appropriate. Other team members are not informed. Interdepartmental chaos breaks out, all trying to decide who the hell's in charge of what. The ship has no rudder and the sails are all set for different wind directions. Attempts at consensus-building degenerate into anarchy.

The Mafia There's one boss and only one boss. The organizational chart is flat; everyone in reality reports to the boss. There is no team. Nobody does or decides anything without the boss's approval. Restitution for getting out of line is swift and administered publicly, as an example to others. Hollow attempts to convince the employees otherwise are received with cynicism and bitterness. No one in the company is confident of the longevity of their tenure. There is no loyalty. Everyone is a mercenary with an up-to-date résumé.

Is Your Culture a Growth Culture?

No attempt will be made here to prescribe the steps to building a growth culture. It is rooted in the ethics and leadership of the senior management team. It grows with the implementation of management and social practices that adhere to the company's ethics. It blossoms with the everyday interactions among all employees in the company. Is a growth culture flourishing in your company?

Here's another of those pesky self-assessments:

CORPORATE CULTURE SELF-ASSESSMENT

1 = Totally Disagree
2 = Somewhat Disagree
3 = Don't Know
4 = Somewhat Agree
6 = Totally Agree

Table 5.2 Corporate Culture Self-Assessment

The Company:	1	2	3	4	5
Rewards growth-oriented behaviors; compensation and promotions; rewards both individual and team successes					
Deals honestly and effectively with the challenges and crises brought on by growth					
Supports challenges to the status quo; encourages risk-taking and unconventional thinking					
Focuses on the future, not the past; on possibilities, not constraints					
Discourages political bickering					
Stresses development of the individual					
Provides the processes and systems to support growth					
Excels at communications, throughout the organization					
Supports growth, from the very top					
Looks at all reasonable alternatives before taking action					
Instills trust					
Provides meaningful and rewarding work for all its employees					

Table 5.2 (*Continued*)

The Company:	1	2	3	4	5
Empowers employees and gives them responsibility to do their jobs, and holds them accountable					
Encourages employees at all levels to participate in growth initiatives					
Clearly articulates its growth vision to all employees					
Listens to all perspectives from any source					
Has the appropriate organizational structure to support growth					
Quickly removes roadblocks to growth once they are identified					
Encourages teamwork at all levels					
Clearly defines everyone's role					

The "score" really matters, but the threshold is higher than normal. Less than a "B" (80) indicates the need to enhance the company's growth culture.

TEAMWORK 101: THE BASIC COURSE IN GETTING THE MOST FROM EACH OTHER

The senior managers of growth companies are, obviously, members of the most important team, the executive team. And, they are constantly and simultaneously building the teams in their separate organizations. The creation and interaction of teams are constants in growth companies. They are always growing and being reorganized, and their overall effectiveness has a lot to do with determining the ultimate success of the firm.

Team Members Come in All Shapes and Sizes

A major factor for team success is the recognition by everyone that team members vary greatly in their natural approach to conducting business and problem-solving. Should nothing else stick with you from this chapter, if we are successful in creating additional awareness of just how different the team members you work with are, then a major mission has been accomplished.

All the readers at one time or another in their careers have been subjected to one form or another of "personality profiling." Myers-Briggs is probably the best-known example. It has been a staple for consultants and business book authors for at least thirty years, so there must be something to it. Regardless of the labels various analyses come up with, common sense and experience clearly show that human beings apply different approaches in dealing with business issues. The simple recognition of that fact has considerable bearing on just how effective a team is.

In the broadest terms, every team member interacts with the team from one of four general perspectives:

- "Let's get all the facts and analyze them."
- "I know the answer, let's do it my way."
- "Lets all work together to come up with an answer."
- "I've got a gut feeling about what we need to do; let's give it a try."

These perspectives don't completely dominate any team member's approach. Mature managers continually alter their approaches; however, each generally begins from one of these starting points.

The relevance of this awareness is the understanding that fellow team members do not address a given situation the same way you might. Usually the mix of perspectives will deliver the best solution, and each perspective has value for the company.

Clarity of Purpose and Individual Roles

Whether at the company, department, or project level, an effective team requires a clear sense of purpose and direction. Ambiguity as to the reason for the team's existence significantly limits the team's effectiveness. Similarly, there can be no overly dominating players on the team. The team is not about the individual; it is about accomplishing the team's shared objectives. Nothing more effectively and graphically represents this than the T-shirts worn by many athletic teams:

Figure 5.1 Team

Key questions regarding team effectiveness include:

- Does the team have a clear understanding of the vision of the task at hand?
- Do members perceive the goal as being more important than their individual roles?
- Does the team have shared values?
- Is there mutual accountability?
- Do all players have meaningful and contributory roles?

Complementary Competencies and Skills

The team's makeup across two dimensions will impact its effectiveness as well as determine how harmonious the collective effort will be: 1) the similarity of basic competencies and abilities, and 2) the mix of skills and knowledge.

A team functions best when all members possess a similar level of general competence, not necessarily in the subject matter, but basic intellect and management skills. Perhaps the best analogy is a hypothetical baseball scenario where a Single A player is brought up to play in the major leagues. The player's attitude is great, he's appreciative of the opportunity, and he hustles all the time. However, his skill level is simply not on a par with his teammates'. He hits .130 and commits an alarming number of errors in the field. His teammates are supportive for a while, but soon their overall concern about the team's success and desire to win the pennant take over. Animosity develops among the player and his teammates. More important, the players begin to wonder just how dedicated the manager of the team is to winning. In their view, the manager should not tolerate this incompetent performance; after all, it's hurting the team's chances for success.

The analogy makes several points relevant to growth companies:

First, competence should be the only real criteria in determining who belongs on the team. Teams have goals and tasks to accomplish ranging from running the company to implementing a project. The only reason the team exists is to accomplish the goals, and insuring the collective competence of team members is the only way the goals will be achieved.

Second, extraneous team member qualities such as desire and work ethic may be admirable and marginally beneficial to the team, but they do not replace ability. All team members must be the best at what they do.

Third, a truism, a chain is only as strong as its weakest link. Team members may try to "cover" another's incompetence, but that distracts them from their own responsibilities. A weak team member's "errors" eventually reduce the entire team's chances for success.

Fourth, team leaders who do not deal effectively with incompetence soon lose the respect of the other team members. If that occurs, the team's effectiveness is minimized.

In addition to the requisite subject matter and functional skills and knowledge, team members should ideally complement each other with other innate capabilities, mostly derived from the personality types identified earlier in the chapter. The operative word is complement, not dominate.

- The *"Let's get all the facts and analyze them"* members bring orderliness and rational thinking to the team. They force the team to deal with facts. They want numbers. They demand logical and sequential analysis.

- The *"I know the answer, let's do it my way"* members serve as lightning rods. They force the other team members to think for themselves and to challenge. Once the best collective idea is conceived, they will become forceful advocates throughout the company.

- The *"Let's all work together to come up with an answer"* members will force discussion and consensus-building. They referee heated discussions and bring the group's focus back on the overall goals.

- And, the *"I've got a gut feeling about what we need to do; let's give it a try"* team members are idea-generators. They test conventional wisdom and counterbalance their "only the facts" teammates.

None of these approaches is totally effective or ineffective on its own. But, dominance of any one of them will not lead to optimum team results. The interaction of all of them stimulates sound thinking, good planning, and thorough execution and also provides a powerful advantage for companies and teams that pull them all together.

Reaching Consensus, or Not

Management teams do not have the luxury their political equivalents enjoy. There are no "minority reports" or the "now we'll hear from the opposition" statements. The team reaches a decision, announces it, and, hopefully, moves forward in solidarity to implement the solution. But, what about the team members who were outvoted or whose ideas were not adopted?

The key to solidarity is not that consensus was reached, but how it was reached. Team members come out of the meeting with one of two attitudes:

- A positive feeling that all ideas were heard, that meaningful debate was fostered, and that although "my idea" did not triumph, it was given a fair hearing. Its merits were addressed but, in the team's view a better idea was adopted.
- There are clear winners and losers. The winners gloat; the losers pout. The winners make sure the rest of the company knows they prevailed in a "contest." The losers make sure the rest of the company knows the "contest" was unfair and they will "get even" in future "contests."

The positive or negative implications to the company of the two attitudes are obvious. Therefore, the challenge to teams is that they reach "consensus" in such a way that when the meeting ends, the first scenario develops.

The answers lie in the unity of purpose of the team. Temporarily setting aside the issues of ugly political and turf issues addressed in a later chapter, if the team is truly determined to do what's best for the company, understands the vision, and wants to achieve it, the situation will take care of itself.

The fortunate thing about growth companies is that many of the fractious behaviors present in larger, more established companies have yet to show themselves...and, hopefully, they never will. The team members have not yet developed destructive political and ego agendas.

If coming from a positive perspective, the team will instinctively adopt the following rules of order in its deliberations:

- There are no winning or losing individuals or cliques; only the company wins or loses.
- There are no bad ideas, just better ones.
- It's not personal; never has been, never will be.
- Every idea is given a fair hearing; nothing is dismissed out of hand.
- What is said here stays here.
- Thou shalt not speak negatively about another team member.

Information Is Power . . . to Be Used Positively

In the entrepreneurial stage, teamwork was unavoidable. Hourly and daily collaboration was the nature of how business was conducted. All team members were involved in almost everything as functional and departmental structures took shape and matured.

Team communications are discussed in the next section, but here the issue is the subtlety of how information is used to enhance or diminish team effectiveness.

As companies grow, it is impossible to share information like in the early days. There's simply too much of it. Growth naturally brings specialization and distinct departments. The business functions develop their own subplans, and dozens of activities of their own are going on at any one time. No one person can keep up, nor should anyone try.

The senior management team members must rely on each other to act as funnels and screens for information, providing each other with what each needs to know in order to guide the company and make good decisions. This mutual dependency is critical to the success of the team. Any overt or covert attempts to withhold information lead to bad decisions, mistrust, and general disharmony within the team.

Reasons for withholding information vary, but team members and the team as a whole must be constantly vigilant to insure that they are getting the information they need from each other in order to function as a cohesive unit.

Reasons for a lack of complete disclosure could include:

- A lack of confidence. A team member may not believe that he made the best decision or performed totally effectively. Telling the "whole story" could be embarrassing to the individual or his department.
- Fear . . . of deriding comments from other team members, primarily the team leader.

- A desire to not be challenged, related to the first two.
- The biggie: a sense that withholding information preserves or establishes a position of power and/or control within the team.

Information is power. It is most powerful when shared and blended with other information from other team members. When information is shared, the team makes the best possible decisions for the company. Anything short of complete and honest disclosure by all team members should not be tolerated.

Nourishing the Team

Like anything else that is a living and breathing entity, the team requires constant attention and care to insure its ongoing effectiveness and viability. All team members, not just the leader, share this responsibility and should actively "feed and water" the team and their teammates.

A curious phenomenon occurs as companies grow. In a small company the executives intuitively sense the needs, frustrations, and victories of their teammates. It may be because they work so closely together, and all triumphs and tragedies affect everyone. Whatever the reason, a mutual support system exists.

The phenomenon we speak of is the withering away of that support system as the company grows. Maybe the executives get too busy. Perhaps the "band of brothers" is not the same group that originally ran the company. Could it be that everyone has become too important in their own minds to recognize the needs of others?

This is not a "Can't we all just get along and sing 'Kumbaya'?" issue. Team effectiveness is dependent on a certain level of mutual respect and support. Without a foundation of trust and respect, a team finds it difficult to sit in a room together, much less accomplish anything meaningful.

How do team members maintain a nourishing environment? A few suggestions:

- Communicate freely, openly, and honestly.
- Acknowledge others' successes.
- Show interest in others' functions and departments.
- Praise individuals in the peers' organizations when they deserve it.
- Offer support when others encounter a professional bump in the road.
- Offer more support when they encounter problems in their personal lives.

A Final Pep Rally

Teams are about winning! Growth companies are about winning! If a team believes it's going to win, its chances of success go up exponentially. The senior management team faces a never-ending series of ups and downs, successes and failures, good days and bad days. But, the impact of a winning and positive environment can't be minimized. It creates winners. It builds camaraderie and positive synergy. It helps the team withstand adversity and it becomes a habit. It's contagious. Catch it!

Communications: The Mechanics

"What we have here is a failure to communicate"...from the Paul Newman movie *Cool Hand Luke* as we recall. How true.

In the last section we established the fact that the volume of information in a growth company is overwhelming. That raises the questions of "Who needs what?"; "How much do they need or want?"; "How is it best communicated?"; "When do they need it?" This chapter addresses those questions as well as some suggested communications techniques to improve the information flow both within the team and with other audiences.

We're All Different

And that is no truer than when applied to communications skills and the need for information. Some executives are blessed with both superb verbal and written communications abilities. Many others are more effective at one than the other. Those individual strengths and weaknesses can be managed as an asset or they can become a liability to the team's ability to communicate. This discussion assumes that senior executives possess a higher proficiency than most people in either verbal or written communications skills. Though the two skills are not mutually exclusive, they'll be treated that way.

The Talkers These individuals possess very well developed verbal skills. They are articulate, easily spontaneous on their feet, and have that wonderful ability to turn the most complex issues into understandable "sound bites." It's likely that they are good negotiators. Left to their natural tendencies, they would rather meet personally with a group or individual or make a phone call rather than write an e-mail or a letter.

The Writers They are comfortable with e-mails and correspondence. Writing comes easily to them, and they formulate their thoughts better on paper than in real-time dialog. They are probably effective PowerPoint presenters; that format allows them to utilize their organizational and writing strengths.

Talkers want to talk and listen; writers want to write and read. With these different communications preferences, intrateam information flow presents challenges.

Streamlining Intrateam Communications

Information flow among team members generally falls into two categories: 1) "official" information that originates with the team leader or other team members and addresses formal activities and actions that the team is working on; 2) "unofficial" information shared by team members that consists of items of general interest, requests for input and review, and so on.

"Official" Information The team should collectively determine its information requirements and the format of how it wants to communicate. Left to individual preferences, team members will deliver anything and everything from a spontaneous verbal report to voluminous narrative documentation. With such disparity, not only will team productivity decline as it attempts to deal with too much/too little information, it incites conflicts. The "talkers" feel slighted if the group focuses on documentation; the "writers" are offended if spontaneous discussion carries the day.

The critical objective is not the avoidance of hurt feelings. The goal is to insure that communications guidelines and expectations enhance efficient and effective decision-making. Whatever the group sets as its expectations is fine. It's inconsequential as to whether the team chooses to accept all information in written or verbal format. However, the team must define its communications expectations in order to not create a major distraction from the tasks at hand.

"Unofficial" Information Senior management in growth companies suffers from information overload. The blessing of the e-mail and the Internet is their ability to deliver incredible amounts of information in real time. The curse is, there is so much of it. Team members have little control over information sent from external sources, but they have a lot of control over what they send to each other.

Team members should strive to not burden their counterparts with voluminous amounts of superfluous information. If an issue or topic requires that much data exchange, it should be put in the "official" bin for full discussion by the team.

These suggestions and, in fact, the whole topic itself, may seem rudimentary and juvenile for a book directed at growth company executives. However, such seemingly simple concepts have a disproportionate impact on how well the team and company function.

Use Your Best Communicators

Team members possess different communications talents. Sometimes the particular skills required for a given situation are not resident in the team member under whose responsibilities the issue falls. A sales executive may need to give a prepared speech before a trade association. The speech requires a great deal of research and concise, targeted writing... but this executive is a "talker." She is perfectly capable of delivering the speech, but will have to stretch to put it together. Why shouldn't the human resources executive who happens to be an excellent writer pitch in?

There's no reason the HR executive shouldn't. It's probable that a growing company has not acquired internal writing talent. The money spent to have the speechwriting outsourced could be put to much better use elsewhere in the company.

We are not naïve regarding the personal dynamics of the senior management team. Neither are we unaware of how closely these team members worked together when the company was in a start-up mode. It's difficult to "go back," but talent-sharing, not just related to communications, but to other skills, can and should remain a characteristic of the senior management team... even when it has grown and the executives have become very "important."

Efficient Communications Suggestions

- E-mails should be no longer than one "screen-full"; utilize bullet points and short sentences. No long narrative paragraphs.
- Briefing Papers should be no longer than two pages. No smaller than 12-point type. Short paragraphs and lots of bullet points. If they are an essential part of a meeting, they should be distributed no later than twenty-four hours prior.
- Meeting minutes are absolutely mandatory! Utilize administrative support to document all meetings, highlighting major points, commitments, and due dates for action. If the matter is confidential and too sensitive for the usual chronicler, a team member should document the session. Minutes should be distributed within twenty-four hours.

- PowerPoint: Become proficient in its use. Whether used for presentations, handouts, or general communications, it's an excellent tool for organizing and presenting ideas concisely.

Insuring that the right information gets to the right people at the right time is vital to a growth company. The senior management team must set the standard for communications flow by:

- Initiating regular two-way communication with all levels in the organization
- Beginning and concluding meetings on time, particularly those with all the troops
- Diligently following up on action items and commitments made in meetings
- Talking about what's important. Long, detailed ramblings severely diminish communications effectiveness (translation: People quit listening)

Inevitable Growth

Success brings growth. Growth brings complexity. Complexity requires a more structured work environment. The structured work environment entails the development of functional departments with increasing specialization and departmental-centric processes and procedures. The company is evolving from an "all for one, one for all" operation to one of a collection of rather independent work groups, each with its own distinct responsibilities. It's moving from a world where a small number of generalists handled everything to one of departmental specialists, each focused on accomplishing discrete goals. How does the company retain a corporate unity of purpose?

The Big Bang

To adopt another analogy, this time from the astrophysicists: Growth companies experience their own "big bangs." From a relatively tight and condensed core, the company suddenly explodes. Though not quite as dramatic as the formation of the universe, a company's "big bang" has the same tumultuous characteristics.

- Everything is initially immensely concentrated in a few people in a small organization.
- Then the "big bang": Growth is dramatic and rather sudden, and "matter" (in a company's case: people, duties, and activities) explodes in all directions.

- The "matter" begins to reunite, not in galaxies and novas, but as functional departments.

The challenge is not only surviving the explosion, but reuniting the "matter" in functional departments in such a way that there is no significant loss of the energy and focus that was present prior to the "big bang."

Silos and Bubbles

The visual representation customarily assigned to business functions is that of silos. The image jumps immediately into one's mind: tall and imposing; concrete cylinders of massive strength; thick walls that insure that nothing moves from cylinder to cylinder. And, we all know those departmental silos: marketing, sales, Management Information Systems (MIS), finance, operations, production, and human resources, among others.

Those images capture the intracorporate environment that growth companies must avoid at all costs. Most readers are very familiar with such environments. They are typical of large, established corporations. Though large companies constantly reorganize and introduce novel management practices, the cylinders never, ever go away. The large companies have too much inertia and ingrained cultural history to avoid or solve the problem. However, growth companies have the opportunity to avoid the malaise of silos.

If silos represent what is to be avoided, what best captures the desired structural vision? Our recommendation: bubbles.

Once the laughter subsides, please give the bubbles imagery a fair hearing. Bubbles are interlocking. They change in size relative to one another. The walls are thin and transparent. Are those not positive characteristics for functional organizations? (For the cynics among you, no, we did not include the bubbles bursting metaphor; bubbles may burst, but silos explode!)

We will not attempt state the benefits of bubbles versus silos; they are obvious and intuitive to senior managers. However, following are recommended "management" and "social" practices that reinforce the company's unity of purpose and minimize the development of noncommunicating, noncoordinating, self-centered departments.

Suggested Management Practices

Careful, Very Careful Design of Compensation Plans Dozens of books have been written about senior management compensation, and they identify hundreds of designs and schemes. Not to minimize any of those ideas, but some things in business life just aren't that complicated.

Compensation drives behaviors. When you identify the desired behaviors, then you pay someone for behaving that way. The challenge is not how the compensation is delivered; the accountants and tax attorneys are perfectly capable of working that out. The real challenge is clearly defining the desired behaviors and insuring that those behaviors are what you really want. Lucrative financial incentives will absolutely make them happen, so be careful about what you wish for.

The most common executive compensation plans acknowledge the achievement of both company and departmental objectives. That's a reasonable approach and forms the foundation for the following recommendations. But, the special needs of growth companies require a good deal more imagination in the design of compensation plans than those found in more established companies. The critical need for interdepartmental coordination and cooperation necessitates strong consideration of weighting the plans more heavily toward the achievement of companywide goals.

Growth companies, no matter their bulk and revenue base, are fragile by definition. The slightest functional-centric thinking can put the company in disarray very quickly.

- Too high a sales volume inundates the company's production or fulfillment capability and/or burns up too much of the capital reserve ... and the sales VP gets a huge bonus.
- Too high a margin goal makes the company's prices uncompetitive in the marketplace ... and the marketing VP gets a huge bonus.
- Stringent systems implementation goals disrupt the company's customer service capabilities because of training requirements or systems downtime ... and the IT VP gets a huge bonus.
- Ambitious hiring plans exceed the company's ability to absorb new workers ... and the HR VP gets a huge bonus.

The list is endless and illustrates the significant interdependence of all departments on each other. Until the company becomes more stable, it is best served by having incentives for senior and middle management primarily focused on companywide goals: corporate profitability, revenue, growth, overall expense reduction, gross margin, and customer retention, to name the most prominent.

Communications, Forced If Necessary The natural and daily communications present at start-up disappear during growth. Functional departments evolve, and there is more than enough to do just keeping up with the day-to-day challenges within each department. As a group, the senior management team members must insist on having meaningful and ongoing communications among themselves.

We discussed information flow earlier in this chapter and looked at some mechanics for making communications easier. However, here we're addressing attitude and desire. If the proper compensation plans are in place, team members should naturally have an interest in other teammates' accomplishments and challenges . . . and, most important, in how the other departments' operations and decisions affect their organizations and the company as a whole.

The crisis management mode, which is ever-present in growth companies, makes interdepartmental communications difficult. No matter how good everyone's intentions are, communications among the whole team always seem to be relegated to a low-priority status. If so, the leader is responsible for insuring that the team communicates and remains focused on the company's well-being as a whole.

Regularly scheduled and well-organized team meetings are the best tonic when departments begin to go astray.

Insure that Middle Management Spreads the Gospel The previous comments address the senior management team, but insuring that middle management is equally committed to the common good of the company is critically important. Middle management runs the daily operations of the company. Silo-like thinking here is no more acceptable than in senior management.

The daily course of business calls for all sorts of interdepartmental actions. Task forces and project teams are created on a needs basis all the time. The senior team should observe as many of these meetings as time allows. The goal is not to drop in and share "wisdom from above," but to promote and demonstrate interfunctional cooperation. Recognize efforts to work things out, and make note of any departmental-centered, selfish attitudes and actions.

Though middle management ad hoc committees and task forces are useful and necessary, their attention is centered on the specific problem or task at hand, and they have little time to deal with broader communications and coordination issues. We highly recommend that middle managers be encouraged to create their own team and forum for identifying and solving interdepartmental problems . . . or, more important, for taking steps and making recommendations to preempt problems before they occur.

Middle management is a huge repository of knowledge about how business is actually conducted. It knows what works and what doesn't. It is closer to the customers and employees than the executives. If senior management sets the proper cooperative tone, the men and women in middle management determine on a daily basis if the company is building silos or bubbles. Don't overlook their ability to significantly contribute to the unity of purpose of the firm.

Suggested Social Practices

Acknowledge Conflict and Deal with It Effectively Few things are more distracting, disruptive, or counterproductive than the effect of grudges and the desire to "get even." Conflicts are as inevitable in a company as they are in any group consisting of more than one human being. Personalities, backgrounds, and professional and departmental differences are constant sources of potential conflict in a company. It's real, it's not going away, and senior management must deal with it both within their team and in other teams.

Teams and companies that do not deal effectively with conflict are creating unnecessary obstacles and challenges. Frankly, there's enough to do, usually too much, for anyone to mope around or contemplate revenge. This makes no contribution to the company; in fact, it takes something away. Every ounce of energy given to such thoughts represents lost opportunities. For example, that energy could be spent in productive thinking, perhaps even creating a breakthrough idea that could catapult the business beyond current expectations.

Every member of the team has the personal responsibility to acknowledge conflict as being natural and expected. And, the atmosphere the team creates for its interaction must allow for conflict and provide an environment for its resolution. Consider the following suggestions for creating that environment.

Stuart Levine, in his article "Managing by Agreement: The New MBA," lays out a straightforward process for dealing with conflict.[1] We have found none better.

> ***Developing the Attitude of Resolution*** This attitude is the place of beginning, a critical first step. This will not happen at once. It will take time to change the way you think. This is the foundational step. The goal is internalizing the principles.

> ***Telling Your Story*** The second step is telling your story and listening to all stories, including yours. It is about understanding and being understood. If you learn to listen with a careful ear and honor everyone's story about a situation, you take a big step toward getting to resolution.

> ***Listening for a Preliminary Vision of Resolution*** The third step is to start thinking about a resolution that honors all concerns in the situation. It is about shifting from the desire to win and get your way to a vision that everyone can buy into. It comes from a sense of fairness.

This initial vision may change as you gather more information and learn more.

Getting Current and Complete The fourth step demands saying difficult, sometimes gut-wrenching things. It is about articulating what usually goes unexpressed and escaping from the emotional and intellectual prisons that keep us locked in the past. It is a way to face the good and bad in any situation and to experience and grieve for the disappointment of unrealized expectations. It is a way to put all of the detail out on the table and choose those remnants that can be used to weave a new tapestry of resolution.

Seeing a Vision for the Future: Agreement in Principle Now that you have a preliminary vision, along with the information and emotional freedom provided by the completion process, you are ready for the fifth step...reaching an agreement in principle. Having looked at what other people need and noticing the cracks in your righteous position, you are ready to reach a general understanding of the resolution. This is the foundation of a new agreement. You let go of the desire for what you know will not work, and you focus on what will.

Crafting the New Agreement: Making the Vision into Reality In the sixth step you put specifics onto the agreement in principle. You design and construct a detailed vision of the future. You have a map, a formula for the dialogue that will maximize the potential for everyone to obtain his or her desired results. The more time you spend in detailing the desired results, the greater the chance to realize them.

Resolution: When Your Agreement Becomes Reality The seventh and final step is moving back into action. With a new agreement and a quiet, clear mind about the past, you can freely move forward, devoting your energy and intention to currently desired outcomes. You will have a new and profound sense of freedom because you have spoken all the unspeakables. You have completed the past and constructed a clear picture of the future and of the highway that will get you there. You will be empowered by the process. You are resolved.

Bad Apples This is a sensitive issue but one that must be addressed. The team, all members, not just the leader, must sometimes acknowledge that a teammate is continually disrupting the team and reducing its ability to function effectively. Every social organization, be it a management team, a civic group, or a family, has members who are eccentric or difficult to get along with. We're not talking about occasional disagreeableness; we all have our "bad days" every now and then. We're referring to ongoing and habitual words and deeds that measurably reduce team effectiveness.

Very talented people exist who simply are not capable of "working and playing well with others." In a business situation, fellow team members, and ultimately the team leader, must constantly balance the contributions of individuals like this with their negative impact on the team. At some point it becomes clear that team effectiveness must prevail.

The termination or reassignment of bad apples must be an option. It's difficult because the individual may be brilliant at his job. But at some point, the negatives of retaining the person on the team outweigh the benefits.

What Is Said Here Stays Here Executives don't fully comprehend the influence they have on the rest of the organization. Subordinates instinctively believe they don't know all that's going on in the company (which is a fact) and are constantly looking for cues and clues. They look to the senior management team for the insight they are lacking. Good internal communications can ameliorate this situation, but human nature being what it is, subordinates always want to know more.

Therefore, they hang on every word and action of the executives, reading something into or trying to "connect the dots" of things real or imagined of every utterance. And, employees are very perceptive. That, combined with inclinations toward gossip by some, create a situation where senior management must be constantly aware of what they say, to whom they say it, and how they say it.

Few things are more disruptive to a company than the perception by employees that friction and dissonance exist among members of the senior management team. People take sides; the watercooler chatter explodes; employees are seen in twos or threes, murmuring constantly. All those activities and others like them sidetrack employees from what they are supposed to be doing.

The senior management team must consciously display unity of purpose. Disagreements and conflict can and will be part of the decision-making process of the team. Feelings will be hurt occasionally and egos bruised. But when the meeting is over and the team leaves the conference room, they cannot give any indication to employees that anything is amiss related to executive team unity. At times it will require executives to put on a bit of an act or just grin and bear it. And, though personal feelings may be involved, communication to the troops must indicate: "It's just business, nothing personal. Now let's get on with it."

Anything less drains too much energy from the tasks at hand.

Mingling Though running the risk of being accused of creating "forced fun," the senior management team should proactively insure that cross-departmental activities and celebrations are a major part of the social structure of the company.

There's a lot to celebrate and talk about in a growth company; employees are constantly doing good things, big and little. The senior management team should create an environment where the increasingly independent departments come together to meet, socialize, and learn about each other.

It is remarkable how quickly the company grows. One day the company can get everybody together for a pizza in the conference room; seemingly the next day, just a departmental meeting requires the logistical planning of D-Day . . . not to mention what it takes to get the whole company together.

Cooperation is facilitated when people know each other. Terse e-mails zipping back and forth among departments are replaced with phone calls and lunches. Minor problems don't get escalated to management; they just get "handled" so management can spend its time on bigger issues. When the employees use the term "we," it refers to the company, not their department.

Making mingling happen takes effort. It's a pain, and not extending the effort can be easily rationalized; there's always something "more important" to do. However, it pays off in terms of creating an environment that fosters easy and informal communications and moderates the inevitable "us/them" attitudes that form with growth.

THE EVOLVING EXECUTIVE TEAM

As the company grows and evolves, so does the management team. Team members change their roles, learn new skills, and reorganize their places in the organization to deal with the constantly changing requirements of the business. Additionally, new team members are added and some original team members depart. This section looks at two of these changes: 1) the progression from generalists to specialists; 2) the infusion of new team members.

The Senior Management Vets

The original senior management team members can be likened to the grizzled GIs so often stereotyped in World War II movies. They went through training together and have the shared experiences of months in combat. They shared the good times and the bad. They have a sense of camaraderie built only through facing a common threat to their survival.

The vets are a natural clique within a growing company. In fact, they may be company icons. They survived the instability and fragility of the early days and firmly believe, for good reason, that they know how to continue to sustain the company's viability. After all, they did it once; they can continue to do it.

Most of the vets also realize that they must change because the company is changing. And, many of them are able to develop the new skills and competencies required. Some aren't. Most clearly understand that growth creates the need for new and different talent to be brought into the company. Some don't.

No matter the disposition of the vets, how they collectively and individually respond to the shifting requirements of the company directly impacts the company's growth and success, and how quickly and easily it is achieved.

Generalists and Specialists

A growth company's requirements evolve from the need for generalists to needing specialists. The "everybody does everything" world changes to one requiring functional competence. As this evolution proceeds and the original senior management team (the vets) acquire responsibilities over functional-specific duties, they must openly and honestly answer several questions:

- What did the company need from me when I joined it?
- What does it need from me now?
- What will it need from me in the future?
- Are the answers to the three previous questions similar or drastically different from each other?
- Were detailed competency requirements identified and do I have them, or did I obtain the position by default?
- Am I equipped for the functional responsibilities I now have?

These questions in no way assume that the vets are not fully capable of moving from a generalist role to one of departmental/functional responsibility. The questions are suggested as a sanity check. A growth company's demands are very, very different than those of the start-up.

New and Replacement Senior Management Recruits

As the company grows, it is almost certain that additional executives will be added to the team, and some of the vets will be replaced.

The circumstances for replacement will vary, but no matter the impetus, how the team deals with these changes in its makeup will impact its ongoing effectiveness.

Changes in the Team's Historical Comfort Zone Under the best of circumstances, a new team member will alter the environment in which the team functions. The change is equivalent to adding a new member to the family. Old group dynamics change. There's a new personality at the table full of new ideas who's not encumbered with the "legacy" way of thinking. The ability for team members to instinctively anticipate where each other will be on a given issue disappears. New members will challenge things that had been taken for granted in the past. As they say, it's a new day.

Jealousy and Doubt Most executives think of themselves as being highly analytical; thinking machines that coolly and calmly assess information and come to rational conclusions. Since executives are also human beings, we suggest that this is a myth.

Despite intellectually understanding the need for and accepting the fact that a new member is valuable, the vets may harbor conscious or unconscious animosity.

- "She's making as much or more than me; I worked for peanuts for over a year getting this company started."
- "He will never understand what it took to get the company to where it is today."
- "I know she has great credentials, but she would have had to live through the tough days to understand how to lead her department."
- "There's no way he can possibly fit into the way we do things around here."

Rational? No. Inevitable? Yes.

"Fitting In" The vets and the headhunter make a lot of fuss about how a new member will "fit" into the team. We may appear to be the heretics here, but once personal integrity, professional competence, and relevant past work environments (more on that shortly) are established, we don't believe that the "fit" issue is all it's made up to be.

The vets have made the company the success it is. They did lots of things right and made tremendous professional and personal sacrifices to launch the company. Most members of the team forced themselves to improve their professional capabilities. However, no matter how much they tried to avoid it, they also created a rut . . . a rut where creative thinking and new ideas are sometimes difficult to come by and too often dismissed without a fair hearing. Along with the benefits of team members instinctively knowing what the others are thinking comes a certain predisposition against new and novel approaches.

Too much commonality leads to inbred thinking, and the quickest way to eliminate that is by adding new team members who are not constrained by "the way it's always been done." The balance between the old and new is very delicate. There are many good and bad old ideas and an equal number of good and bad new ideas. Egos and emotions are thrown into the mix for good measure.

Sustained profitable growth requires a constant influx of new ideas combined with the old ones that worked so well. New team members "fit" if they have new ideas and stir things up a bit. Competence, integrity, and the ability to bring new thinking to the team should be the only "fit" criteria, with the possible exception of candidates' prior work environment. Bringing in new senior managers who mirror the existing team's age, gender, experience, and cultural background is a sure formula for stifled creativity . . . and for creating a workforce focused on maintaining the status quo, repeating past activities, and insuring that things are done "like we always have done it."

Where Should the Recruits Come From? Conventional wisdom (whatever that is) suggests that as companies grow, they are best served by bringing in executive team members from larger, more established firms. The assumption is that such individuals possess a higher level of management sophistication, are better equipped to develop processes, and possess more refined functional knowledge. While accepting the identified needs, we suggest that growth companies need those competencies plus others just as valuable.

Five candidate sources:

- Entrepreneurs
- Small companies
- Consultants
- Larger growth companies
- Large companies

Each category has its pluses and minuses, but on the whole, individuals who come from larger growth companies are uniquely suited. Coming in second place are consultants.

Entrepreneurs are energetic, resourceful, and immensely flexible. Those qualities are resident in the existing management team. And, an individual's successful track record in a *small company* only proves that he is capable of doing what the growth company has already done...the company has "been there, done that."

Consultants provide viable candidates for additions to the team only if the company has engaged them previously in a consulting role. Growth companies use functional-specific consultants, particularly in the early growth spurt stage. The team has the opportunity to "sample" the consultant's capabilities and determine how well she works with other team members. It is likely she will have executive experience and not only understand the area of expertise on which she is providing counsel, but the "corporate world" as well. Care should be taken by the team to insure that a consultant is not so focused on a topical area that she cannot contribute to the broader challenges of a growth company.

The aforementioned conventional wisdom regarding *executives recruited from large companies* bears scrutiny. Though the necessary skills and knowledge may be present, candidates who have experience *only* in large company environments may be severely mismatched with the needs of a growth company. The reasons are mainly cultural in that the factors and prerequisites for success differ dramatically from those of a growth company. At the risk of stereotyping, success in large companies in part depends on:

- Pedigree
- Political acumen
- Massive support systems
- Massive capital and availability of endless resources
- Personal flair more than substance
- Friends in high places

None of those attributes are of any use to growth company executives, and, in fact, are detrimental to the team's ongoing success.

Last is the category that has the most potential for providing new team members: *larger growth companies*. These candidates share many of the experiences of the veterans yet are likely more aware of what's to come. They've fought the battles and faced the challenges the company has yet to encounter. They've dealt with growth on a larger scale and have succeeded. They share similar cultural values and are not shocked by the inherently hectic and demanding pace.

All the categories have been stereotyped for purposes of explanation. Great candidates can originate from all sources. The team's challenge is to insure that whoever is selected brings the ethics, competencies, and new ideas necessary for energizing the team.

Evolving Loyalties

All growth companies started as entrepreneurships. The entre-preneurs' vision drove the companies, and their charisma and passion attracted many of the early team members and employees. Intense loyalties to the founders developed, and their leadership and untiring devotion to the company and its employees positioned it for what was accomplished.

The company today (or the one that will exist tomorrow) may or may not include the founding team members. The possibility exists the original team members may eventually be outnumbered by the recruits. Therefore, it is imperative that all team members clearly understand the ultimate loyalty...and that is to the company's con-tinuing and ongoing growth and success.

Teammates who have friendships and close professional rela-tionships must realize that other teammates will come and go. To-morrow's team may be drastically different than yesterday's. But, two loyalties exist and must remain constant:

- First, to the employees, who *are* the company, dozens or hundreds of people who depend on the company for their livelihood;
- Second, to the investors who chose to accept the risk of funding an unproven venture.

Those constants alone must always drive loyalty.

OFFICE POLITICS: IS IT MANAGEABLE?

Well, here we are close to the end of the chapter, and we can't put the topic off any longer. Using its most negative connotation, fol-lowing are observations on the impact of office politics in a growth company.

One of the joys of companies in the entrepreneurial stage is that they are so busy and focused on survival that office politics has little opportunity to raise its ugly head. The company is small and singu-larly focused. Communications are open and extensive, both across and up and down the organization. Subtlety is not a descriptor of the company. Disagreements get settled in real time, perhaps with shouting matches, but when it's over, it's over. Machiavellian machi-nations take too much time and effort.

As the company grows and adds more employees one can assume with absolute certainty that a certain percentage, across all levels, will use "politics" to accomplish personal objectives.

What Is Office Politics?

Here's our simple definition: "The practice of using guile, deceit, unearned influence, and manipulation to accomplish personal objectives that may or may not be in the best interests of the company, its owners, or its employees."

This definition intentionally removes positive persuasion, leadership, and communications efforts that benefit the company. It also leaves room for the potential for politics to benefit the company, but if it does, it is purely coincidental. Its primary objective is for personal benefit.

How does it show itself?

- Senior and middle managers throw their weight around to stroke their egos.
- Employees spread gossip and rumors to enhance their position among peers.
- Cliques form to enhance their power and position within the company.
- Information is withheld and/or manipulated for personal gain.
- Credit is taken for work done by others.
- Individuals court the favor of their bosses using things other than their contributions to the company.
- Individuals pit one employee against another for self-aggrandizement.

In a perfect world, companies would not have to deal with internal politics, but companies are made up of human beings with all their frailties and shortcomings. Political behaviors are inevitable, so companies simply must deal with them as effectively as possible, and that starts at the top.

Don't Provide a Support System

Senior managers are often more guilty of *allowing* political shenanigans than of practicing them. Not that they are absolved from all blame, but for the most part they simply have more to worry about and have not yet seen the need to expend the energy required if so inclined. However, allowing themselves to be manipulated by and responding positively to politically motivated overtures encourages the culprits.

Senior management personnel may not be infected by politics, but they are carriers. They can be the enablers who allow it to thrive in the organization.

Politically motivated individuals behave as they do only because it works. Their self-interests drive their behaviors, and if those behaviors don't work they'll cease them and try something else...maybe even eventually realizing that focusing on the company's best interests presents the best path to achievement of their personal goals.

Just Say No

Don't allow yourself to be lured into behaviors that unconsciously support politically motivated initiatives. Firmly but politely terminate conversations that are going down the wrong path. Obtain second opinions when in doubt about the motivations behind certain words and deeds. Practice the "just the facts" response if approached with hearsay and speculation. Don't take sides until you understand the background.

Office politics is a reality of corporate life. Senior managers would be wise to insure that they are not an inadvertent cause of the problem.

IS THE TEAM REALLY A TEAM? A TEAM EFFECTIVENESS ASSESSMENT

Indicate your agreement/disagreement with the following statements:

1. Totally disagree
2. Somewhat disagree
3. Don't know
4. Somewhat agree
5. Totally agree

Table 5.3 Team Effectiveness Assessment

	1	2	3	4	5
Team members recognize each other's different approaches to problem-solving.					
Team members will alter their personal approaches when it is required for overall team success.					
The TEAM/me perspective is shared by all.					
The team shares a common goal and vision.					
The team has joint and mutual accountability.					
Team members' individual competencies in their areas of expertise are roughly equivalent.					

Table 5.3 (*Continued*)

	1	2	3	4	5
Team consensus is usually achieved.					
If consensus is not achieved, all team members deal with it in a positive manner.					
Team members openly and freely share information among themselves.					
Team members continually work to improve the team's interactions.					
Team members acknowledge each other's personal and departmental accomplishment.					
A winning attitude is pervasive in the team.					
Team members acknowledge and respect others' communications styles.					
Team members respect each other's time constraints and communicate succinctly and briefly, no matter the style.					
Compensation and incentive plans are supportive of teamwork.					
Team members seldom if ever take actions that will disrupt fellow team members' organizations.					
Middle management interdepartmental teams work together effectively.					
The team acknowledges the existence of conflict and deals with it effectively.					
The senior and middle management team have no bad apples.					
The team never allows its disagreements or conflicts to spill into the rest of the company.					
The team insures that everyone in the company knows one another.					
Veterans and recruits work effectively together.					
All team slots are filled.					
The team's ultimate loyalty is to the employers and investors of the company.					

Chapter 6

CHANGING THE EMPHASIS FROM SALES/REVENUE TO MARGIN/PROFITS

THE TRIPLE WHAMO

This chapter is not intended to be an attempt to impersonate a CFO. There are several reasons for not embarking on such a delusional venture, the main one being we're simply not qualified financial gurus.

However, since all the members of the executive team in a growth company are involved with and knowledgeable of "the numbers," as nonfinancial individuals, we will address several issues from an operating and strategic perspective.

Our goal in this chapter is to, rather vividly, point out what should be rather intuitively obvious but sometimes isn't: The bottom line (profitability) of the company is more important than the top line (revenue). The causes for missing out on the obvious are intellectual, attitudinal, psychological, and organizational. We will look at each in this chapter in order to, hopefully, help you avoid the mistakes of many others.

When Revenue Was King

As we have alluded to earlier in the book, sales/revenue/cash are the primary metrics for entrepreneurial companies. Whether the company is relying on self-generated cash or investments/loans, the creation of critical mass in terms of sales volume and revenue is paramount. But, recall the "any customer is a good customer" niche discussion.

The sales/revenue focus is present in all industries, but particularly so in the telecommunications and high-tech worlds of 2000. Billions in investments were made based on the *anticipated* growth of the customer base and revenues, without a glimmer of profitability for years and years, if ever. Speed to market, revenue growth, and a sexy product were the major investment criteria. Dot-com companies absorbed these billions only to go under, and though some did establish significant revenue streams, few ever came within shouting distance of profitability.

But those days are gone, and today's growth companies must demonstrate rather quickly that they can not only produce revenue, but profits, and do it in a relatively short time. It seems that investors have returned to the "good old days" of investing in businesses that actually have a reasonable chance of making real money. That reality stimulates a rather natural progression in growth companies in emphasis from a revenue to a profit emphasis.

Reality Sets In

Profitability requires a lot more than a shift in emphasis. There are many moving parts, as everyone knows. Expenses have a *little* to do with it, but growth companies are in an ever-expanding mode, and expansion is costly. Only so much can be done with expense management when the company is busily acquiring customers, hiring people, and expanding its infrastructure.

The shift in emphasis to the bottom line (profitability) may begin with more scrutiny of the nature and profitability of the sales that are being made. If the company has stressed revenue, it likely created an expectation in the sales channels of "sales at any cost." Since most sales organizations of entrepreneurial/early growth spurt companies were not compensated on margin, there was little incentive to focus on anything except making the sale...any sale. Discounts were requested and likely granted. Special promotions became the norm, not the exception. Sales expenses crept up because growing the customer and revenue base was all important.

Efforts at margin management were probably focused on the "buy side" of the equation. Purchasing (as purchasing has and will always do) hammered suppliers to obtain the best possible cost of goods. However, little attention was given to the "sell side" of the margin equation.

The company attracted any kind of customer, but regrettably, some customers were acquired and retained at a terribly high cost. Some sales channels' costs of acquisition went through the roof: more sales reps were required than anticipated; "close" rates on telemarketing calls were below target; there was a requirement to boost agent compensation; nonbudgeted advertising expenses crept in, and so on. The combination of reduced prices demanded by the customers and greater selling effort required to acquire them dwarfed the operating expenses forecast in the budget. To make matters worse, some customers required significantly more support during implementation of the sale. And, once implementation was complete, the ongoing customer service requirements of some customers went far beyond what anyone had anticipated. None of these additional costs were anticipated in the budget.

Revenues are on target, but all of a sudden the company finds itself hit with a triple whamo that's deteriorating profitability:

- Revenues per customer have declined due to aggressive discounting and promotions.
- Sales expenses have gone up; you have to have more customers than anticipated if the projected revenue-per-customer goes down.
- General & Administrative (G&A) expenses go up due to higher than expected costs of implementation and customer support.

The Whamo Arrives

Following is a scenario that emphasizes just how the interaction of pricing, sales practices, and G&A costs can combine to decimate a thriving enterprise and force a shift in emphasis from sales/revenue to margin/profit.

A Scary Hypothetical Scenario ACME Enterprises is a poster child for rapidly growing service companies. It has revenues of $10 million and will end the year with an $800,000 operating profit. Times are good. The employees are fired up, and the investors are happy. The executive team will get nice bonuses.

The company has thrived on sales. In a fairly immature market, its aggressive sales and pricing strategies have allowed it to pick off much of the "low-hanging fruit"...those prospects that offer the most potential for least effort. Margins have been strong enough to allow steep discounting. The sales channels, be they direct sales, third-party distributors, telemarketing, or other means, are well compensated, a little fat and happy, and content that headquarters interferes little in their activities as long as the sales quota is met.

Flush with its success, the company has paid little attention to the shifting sands on which that success is built. Competition is heating up, and sales aren't quite as easy to close as they once were. Discounting is on the increase. Operations is just beginning to squawk about the increasing implementation and customer support demands. As they put it, "Every damn deal is different! Do we ever sell the standard product with the standard support?"

The company believes that doing more of what it always has done is the key to continuing growth and success: Sell more! Next year's budget calls for an even more aggressive sales push. Prices are lowered, but this will reduce overall margins by only 1 percent. Additional selling initiatives, sales incentives, and advertising will increase sales expenses only 2 percent, up to 12 percent of revenue. That's only $440,000, and these adjustments will increase next year's revenues by 20 percent, from $10 million to $12 million. $440,000 invested to gain $2 million more in revenue. What a deal!

Yeah...what a deal. In addition to the changes explained above, there was one little surprise. Due to continued internal complexity, lack of standardization, and the need to live up to the sales organization's various promises for post-sale support, G&A as a percentage of revenue grew from 20 to 22 percent. It simply cost more to deliver the product or fulfill the service and support the customer than was anticipated.

As the accompanying before and after P&Ls show, the great $2 million increase translated into a year-over-year decrease of operating profits of $440,000...a 55 percent reduction.

ACME ENTERPRISES P&L COMPARISON

Table 6.1 ACME Enterprises P&L Comparison

	Current Fiscal Year	Next Fiscal Year	Next vs. Current
Revenue	$10,000,000	$12,000,000	+ $2,000,000
COG $	$6,200,000	$7,560,000	+ $1,360,000
COG %	62%	63%	+ 1%
Gross Margin $	$3,800,000	$4,400,000	+ $600,000
Gross Margin %	38%	37%	− 1%
Sales Expense $	$1,000,000	$1,440,000	+ $440,000
Sales Expense %	10%	12%	+ 2%
G&A Expense $	$2,000,000	$2,640,000	+ $640,000
G&A Expense %	20%	22%	+ 2%
Operating Profit $	$800,000	$360,000	− $440,000
Operating Profit %	8%	3%	− 5% absolute (−55%) relative

Build Your Own Spreadsheet

We urge executives, particularly those whose companies are emerging from the early growth spurt stage and entering adolescence, to build this simple spreadsheet. Use ACME or your own company's numbers. Tweak the variables to vividly see the impact of the shift in emphasis from sales/revenue to margin/profits.

The Shift

With the "triple whamo," the company arrives at some basic conclusions:

- All customers/revenue/sales are not equal.
- All products are not equal.

What does the company do with this newfound awareness?

ALL CUSTOMERS/REVENUE/SALES, AND PRODUCTS, ARE NOT EQUAL

Larry Selden and Geoffrey Colvin in their book *Angel Customers & Demon Customers* put forth their "150–20 rule":[1]

- 150 percent of companies' profits come from less than 20 percent of their customers.
- The bottom 20 percent may lose money equal to 150 percent of profit.
- The remaining 60 percent of customers make up the difference.

(Note: The figures are not supposed to add up to 100 . . . You have very profitable customers contributing excessive profits, with the bottom 20 percent basically canceling those out. And the remainder contribute whatever profit was actually made.)

Mitch Rosenbleeth of Booz-Allen & Hamilton recounts a recent experience with a client where 30 percent of a company's customers created 200 percent of its profits. Half of the customers produced little profit, and the remaining 20 percent "destroyed profits."[2]

In other words, at least some elements of the "whamo" afflict many if not most companies. Our experience indicates that this is particularly true for early-stage growth companies for many of the reasons detailed in the previous chapter.

In addition to the inbred and cultural emphasis on sales volume and revenue growth, these companies are often slow to recognize the factors that lead to unprofitable revenues. And, though the concept of "customer profitability" has existed for over ten years, and huge customer relationship management (CRM) and data-mining advances are providing new tools, many rapid-growth firms have not benefited from them.

Unprofitable customers, similar to churning customers, are another one of those silent killers that can prove fatal if not detected and jettisoned early on.

What Makes for Unprofitable Customers?

A main contributor, in a word, is averaging. Conventional wisdom, habit, and/or a lack of processes and technological capability drive most companies to "averaging" in their various analyses. It's logical, prudent, and can yield meaningful conclusions, but only if wide disparities do not exist with what's being averaged. Be it gross margin calculations, prorating of overhead expenses, or distribution of sales/marketing expenses, averaging can produce very distorted numbers; this distortion, again, is related to the degree of disparity among the elements being averaged.

Potential "Problem-Maskers" *Average Gross Margin:* Though addressed separately in the next section, disparate product/product line margins have obvious implications on profitability. Different production/purchasing costs and other inherent "cost-of-goods/services" elements may drastically distort average margins. And, with different products producing different margins, the profitability of products purchased by a customer will vary greatly.

Average Sales/Marketing Expense: Simply dividing all sales/marketing costs by orders or products sold produces an average that is likely quite unrepresentative of customers who soak up an either unusually high or low share of the sales/marketing costs. This is especially true if multiple channels (direct sales, telemarketing, etc.) are utilized.

Average Purchase: Some customers buy in large quantities, requiring only one order to be processed and only one bill rendered. Others are just the opposite: many small orders and many bills. And collectively, all of the smaller multiple purchases may not equal a fraction of a large user's order.

Average Support Costs: This is perhaps the most difficult element to get a handle on. However, whether by design or otherwise, customers require a disproportionate share of support. Some never call with a complaint or service problem. Others call weekly. Some large customers may demand higher levels of service in return for their business; others don't. Assuming that all customers require the same amount of attention, and thus should share an equal allocation of the costs, is refusing to acknowledge the obvious.

Average Days of Receivables: Everyone measures this. All businesses have their 30/60/90/120-day reports. Though an indicator of a company's general financial health, do you really know, at the individual customer level, who's either not paying you or paying you late? And, do you know what it's costing you in profits?

Beware: Major Accounts

All sales organizations and most companies covet major accounts. To stereotype, these are large customers providing lots of revenue; they're prestigious, and everyone gets all giddy when they are acquired. A question that is often not asked, however, is whether or not this blessing called a major account will be profitable?

Perhaps bursting the bubble that surrounds high-revenue accounts, we posit that far too many of them have the "problem-maskers" identified above. The following is a representation of a company that hailed its major account programs and urgently stressed the desire to add more to its customer list.

- Higher sales commissions were paid to sellers who acquired major accounts.
- A separate sales force was dedicated to acquiring major accounts; this move was necessary in order to provide the resources required to develop complex proposals and respond to bid requests.
- Special sales collateral was developed to assist in acquiring new major accounts.
- A discount pricing schedule was developed especially for major accounts; some discounts offered went beyond the schedule.
- Major accounts, as a group, purchased the least profitable products sold by the company.
- The major accounts demanded and received dedicated service personnel.
- The major accounts consistently requested product delivery intervals shorter than those normally offered by the company.
- Sometimes the smallest breakdown in service delivery by the company resulted in executive-level complaints from the major accounts.

- The major accounts required a special billing format that the company had to customize and support.
- The major accounts were consistently slow to pay and constantly disputed the bills rendered.

There is no punch line to this story. The company never analyzed to any degree the profitability of its major accounts. Intuitively, everyone realized they were not profitable, but the company continues merrily along, proud of every major account it acquires. It's a good thing it has enough "nonmajor accounts" to pay the bills!

What To Do?

In an ideal world (a world in which some fortunate companies exist), profitability is tracked down to the individual customer. However, the systems and process requirements to provide this granular level of analysis are far beyond the capabilities of many early-stage growth companies. But an "analytical attitude shift" is well within the capabilities of any enterprise.

De-average! Every organization's analytical and systems capabilities are different, but senior management should force de-averaging of key indicators/results as broadly and as deeply across the organization as possible. We think you will be surprised at what can be accomplished simply by asking for it. You may never get to the level of individual customer profitability, but you can certainly move in that direction.

Think in terms of segments or groups, not the whole. Identify the common characteristics among certain customer or prospect groups. Initially you may have to "guesstimate" prorates and loadings; there is a point of diminishing returns for efforts to *precisely* allocate shared costs. But, a zillion-dollar cost allocation system isn't required to develop a reasonably accurate profitability model for the various segments or groups.

Existing Unprofitable Customers Once you get a handle on which customers are profitable and which aren't, the task then becomes to turn the latter into the former. The options available are obvious... increase prices, lower costs, or devise some combination of the two. The goal will be to retain the customer, but only if the level of profit contribution achieves a threshold acceptable to the company.

Ultimately, the prospect of "firing" customers becomes a reality, as referenced in chapter 3. Though completely counterintuitive to growth companies, particularly those in early-stage development, it simply must be addressed. Whether the firings are overt or subtle, it has to be done. Continuing to subsidize a growing base of unprofitable customers can be lethal to sustainable, *profitable* growth.

New Unprofitable Customers? Dealing with a group of unprofitable legacy customers isn't pleasant, but it's necessary in order to solve problems originating from prior sins. However, the sinning cannot continue.

Armed with a better understanding of profitability by groups or segments, the first step is to insure that there are *no* incentives for the sales force to acquire unprofitable customers. It is absolutely critical that the organization not reward behaviors it really doesn't want, and acquiring unprofitable customers is definitely an undesirable behavior.

What about Products?

Companies vary greatly in the number of products they offer, but most have more than one. And, growth companies will likely expand their product portfolios as they mature. A portfolio of products must be managed like an investment portfolio... invest in the winners, divest the losers.

Thomas K. Brown writing in *Bank Director* magazine cites consultants Mercer Oliver Wyman in pointing out the disparity of product line profitability of banks:[3]

- The top 10 percent most profitable products generate 70 percent of overall product profits.
- The bottom 80 percent contribute less than 1 percent of profits.

A midsize service company with which we are familiar had gross margins ranging from 75 percent to minus 30 percent for its various products.

Therefore, if a company has more than one product, the "averaging" of product/product line profitability harbors similar potential for "problem-maskers," as does averaging of customer profitability. And, the product profitability puzzle, interestingly, confounds not only early-stage organizations. Again, according to Robert C. Docters of Booz-Allen & Hamilton, though 93 percent of U.S. companies over $100 million have some sort of automated product profitability system, less than one-third analyze profitability at the level required to develop sound, profit-based product strategies.[4]

If the "big boys" have a problem getting it right, rapidly growing firms find product profitability an even more vexing issue. In addition to generally not having the necessary systems sophistication, they must also contend with additional challenges:

- Early analysis and modeling may have been unsophisticated, and the baseline from which later analysis was conducted is, therefore, flawed.
- Things change . . . due to what the company does. Production, sales, and overhead costs go up or down. Product lines expand and/or are altered.
- Things change . . . due to what others do. Supplier costs go up or down. Prices are adjusted to meet the competition.

Consequently, we have another of those "change" situations: The beginning point may be incorrect and all the variables, internal and external, are constantly in play. A nice solution would be one of those product profitability systems, but few early stage companies do, and from what we observed above, it might not work anyway.

Absent such a system, we suggest the same grouping concept as suggested for determining customer profitability. Key cost variables can be identified and categories defined. However, of critical importance is early recognition that as time passes and more products are developed, the more likely major profitability disparities will evolve.

As observed often in this book, avoiding problems is so much easier than trying to solve them later. All customers/revenue/sales and products are not equal! The euphoria of growth must be moderated with the recognition that the sooner profitability balances selling and product introduction decisions, the more likely growth will be sustained.

Alternative Approaches

The following identifies some rather unorthodox approaches to looking at a company's financials. We recommend that senior management review these approaches and others with an eye toward putting more focus on the ultimate goal—profitability. There's a lot more to be seen and pondered than just the top line.

REM In his book *Creating and Sustaining Company Growth*, James B. Hangsteffer introduced the term REM, or revenue margin. The theory behind REM is the author's contention that the current concept of gross margin is obsolete; that it is a holdover from the Industrial Age, when the cost of goods was the primary determinant of revenue generation. The author's implicit assumption is that the art of marketing had yet to develop, and price, governed by cost of goods, was the sole factor in the generation of revenue.[5]

REM is calculated as follows:

$$REM = \frac{COGS + Sales\ /\ Marketing\ Expenses + Customer\ Support\ Expenses}{REVENUE}$$

In short, the formula captures all product delivery costs, separating them from the true "overhead" of the company. We believe that this concept has value for high-growth companies. It gives the company a yardstick by which to measure *all* its revenue creation and retention activities against revenue growth.

Additionally, calculating REM would provide more of a granular look when companies compare various product lines, customer segments, and geographic markets. The accounting required to extract currently commingled costs would be cumbersome, and completely discrete identification of costs at the granular level suggested may not be cost-effective. However, REM at its highest level offers new insight for the senior management team.

ABC Tom Pryor in an article entitled "The Demise of Gross Margin Pricing" utilizes a similar philosophy, but attacks the issue from another direction.[6] Pryor defines his ABCs below:

A. A Bill of Activity is created that lists all the activity costs directly traceable or consumed by the product, service or customer.
B. Non-traceable business sustaining activities, such as "Do Monthly Closing," are then allocated to the Bill of Activity.
C. Traceable costs + Non-traceable costs + Profit = Sales Price.

Pryor approaches the issue from the perspective of developing a price by identifying as many direct costs as possible (similar to REM), adding prorated indirect costs, then adding the required profit margin. Though price-focused, ABC acknowledges the need to understand the COG, selling, and customer support costs as a single entity.

REM and ABC may not be suitable for all companies for a variety of reasons. However, they spur creative thinking by high-growth companies into developing alternative ways to look at the numbers.

SALES VERSUS MARKETING: BALANCING REVENUE AND PROFIT PRIORITIES

The business literature is rich with observations of and commentaries about one of the classic functional debates—that of the roles of sales and marketing. However, we will only crack this Pandora's box a little, with a focus on implications to a company's revenue or profit orientation. So, let's explore the dynamics described in the Whamo section a little more closely.

Roles

We will take the liberty of using stereotypical perspectives of the sales and marketing organizations. Though there is some risk in dealing with stereotypes, we believe they accurately portray the love/hate relationship between these two vital business functions.

Sales: It is the powerful and necessary darling of early-stage, high-growth companies. By definition, the sales organization had to be successful at bringing in customers and developing the company's revenue stream. As postulated earlier, it is highly likely that sales was one of the strongest, if not the most powerful, departments in the company. It was delivering new customers and acquired the internal power that rightfully accompanied its success.

Sales' job is to sell, to sell the products it has been provided at the prices the company has established.

Marketing: Among other things, it is the keeper of the margin keys. As one of its most important responsibilities, marketing establishes prices and monitors (or should) the all-important "sell side" of the gross margin of the business. Coupled with stringent purchasing/production cost management, marketing must bring focus to the sometimes no-fun analysis of profitability emphasis to balance the sexier, more glamorous revenue emphasis.

At an earlier stage in the company's evolution it is likely that sales had a great deal to do with setting prices, probably because the marketing function had yet to mature. Our experience shows that in emerging high-growth companies, the margin maintenance responsibilities of marketing, though perhaps the most important of its functions, take a backseat to mandatory but relatively less strategic duties: advertising, public relations, sales collateral, and the like.

If the sales organization has historically been the major player in the establishment of pricing and discounting policies, it will be very reluctant to give up those prerogatives. Sales' job has been to sell, and setting competitive prices and offering appealing discounts to the sellers is a sure way to increase sales volume and revenue. And, that goal may well have been paramount in the past. However, at some point the organization will begin to emphasize profitability, and, barring the fairly rare situation where sales compensation is based more on profitability than revenue, leaving pricing and discounting decisions in the hands of the sales organization is, simply, a mistake.

Checks and Balances

Pricing is one of those processes that deserves and demands a complete hearing, full disclosure, and active debate. Organizations must constantly assess the strategic value of revenue growth and profitability. The two need not necessarily be mutually exclusive, but in most industries the lower the price, the more you sell; the higher the price, the more profit you make. Though overly simplistic, the vision of a seesaw comes to mind: prices on one side, profits on the other . . . one goes up, the other goes down.

At different stages of a company's evolution, the strategy may favor one over the other (if you can't have both.) Acquiring market share will favor lower prices. A forecast of hard economic times on the horizon will encourage cash accumulation and higher prices and profits. And, of course, competitors have more than a little impact on your pricing policies.

But, no matter the strategic driver at any given time, advocates of both the low price/high sales volume and higher price/higher profit positions should be provided a forum to debate and substantiate their respective points of view, with facts, figures, and analysis.

Clearly the revenue/profit debate seldom produces an obvious "no-brainer" conclusion. There are always holes in the data. Sales can't be sure of the negative or positive impact on volume of a price increase or decrease. Marketing might produce spreadsheets that indicate the impact of a price change, but only if their volume assumptions are accurate. And, what will the competitors do as a result of a price change? It's all a matter of conducting the best analysis possible and applying the aggregate judgment of those involved in making the decision.

However, the point here is that the debate must occur. The analyses must be made. Those who represent "lower price/revenue growth" and others in the "higher price/higher profit" camps must have equal representation and clout in the debate. The outcome should not be preordained, barring some overwhelming strategic imperative. Each side should be prepared to offer its best case and do so. The absence of any compelling fact or argument, on either side, could lead to a less than optimum decision.

The Structure

If the marketing function in the organization is "late-blooming" and junior to the sales organization, the senior management of growth companies must insure that marketing receives the attention it needs during its incubation period. Critical during that incubation period is the determination of organizational structure(s) in which sales and marketing will coexist.

Many variations exist, but we propose one guiding rule regarding the structure of the sales and marketing organizations: Both should report ultimately to an executive whose incentive compensation is equally dependent on 1) the achievement of sales/revenue goals, and 2) the achievement of corporate profitability goals. Any bias at the decision-making level will alter the all-important concept of checks and balances.

Some firms assign both sales and marketing responsibilities to a single executive. This is, perhaps, the structure most aligned with the principles presented. Other companies separate the two functions between two different executives. This simply pushes the checks and balances responsibilities to a higher level, and can make it more difficult to develop and manage the forum described earlier. The CEO, COO, or president may simply not have the time necessary to insure that the revenue/profit debates are fair and productive.

Chapter 7

POSITIONING HR MANAGEMENT AS A STRATEGIC ADVANTAGE

HR: COST CENTER OR STRATEGIC ADVANTAGE, YOU DECIDE

The first discipline introduced in this book addressed the critical role customer loyalty plays in sustaining profitable growth. We also made several recommendations concerning processes and policies to enhance customer loyalty. Every one of those suggestions ultimately relies on the customer-contact employees in your company interfacing efficiently, effectively, and positively with your customers . . . from the customers' perspective.

Though every organization sooner or later discovers just how important customer loyalty is, many do not perceive the critical role HR plays. The best policies and programs created to increase customer loyalty are for naught if the human beings who interface daily with customers are not hired, trained, compensated, and motivated with the customer in mind. In short, happy employees make for happy customers. And, happy employees don't just happen; the environment that nurtures employees' satisfaction with their jobs and enhances their productivity is a result of thoughtful HR strategies developed within the context of the company's overall business plan.

The Evolution of the HR Function

As a business function, HR has evolved significantly in the last forty years. The Personnel Department of the 1960s with its primary role of hiring and firing has given way to the modern HR Organization charged with a multitude of responsibilities. And, in most large, mature companies, HR takes a seat at the executive table with no fewer responsibilities and opportunities for strategic input than its sister functions of operations, marketing, and finance. For many companies HR has evolved from a transactional, tactical orientation to one where it delivers results by translating the business's strategies into HR priorities.

However, even in some more mature firms, even if HR has been given a seat at the planning table, it is still viewed prejudicially as strictly a cost center; an expensive overhead whose budget is one of the first to be cut. Goes to show that "mature" companies don't necessarily think maturely. Though people are the heart and soul of any company's ability to serve its customers, the very organization charged with making sure that the right employees are available with the right training and the right attitudes sometimes becomes a minor player.

Let us state this as forcefully as possible: HR can and must play a major role in the development and implementation of any organization's strategies; anything less will invariably hinder a company's ability to sustain profitable growth.

HR in Growth Companies

Our experience clearly shows that many companies exiting entrepreneurship and enjoying an early growth spurt simply do not make HR a high priority. In fact, there are many similarities between the evolution of HR in growth companies and the general evolution of the function over the last few decades.

As recounted earlier, it's likely that the founders of the business were directly involved in early hiring decisions. As a result, these early hires were very competent and dedicated. Then, the need for new employees grew exponentially as a result of the business's success. So, what do many companies do? They hire a recruiter. Certain employee thresholds are achieved that require regulatory reporting, so an HR specialist is hired to take care of it. Soon employee benefits become an issue; another specialist is hired to handle that. The traditional mentoring and on-the-job training is no longer tenable, so a trainer is hired. After a while there are so many HR folks that a supervisor is hired, the HR manager.

The point: The HR function begins to grow from the bottom up. Tasks and transactions had to be accomplished, and expertise was acquired to handle them. Though most business plans we have seen give at least a passing mention of "high-quality customer service," "a highly motivated employee body," "exceptional employee competencies," "a highly motivated work environment," and so on, the real truth is that most organizations have absolutely no plan to insure that such lofty goals are achieved. Companies simply hire tactical resources to deal with all the problems and hassles that come with all these new employees.

The Path Not Taken

At this point in a company's evolution, one of two paths will likely be embarked upon. For some firms it will be more of what has been previously described. More problems, regulations, lawsuits, and hassles will have to be dealt with; therefore, more HR people will be hired and the organization will continue to grow from the bottom up. Eventually HR will become large enough (if for no other reason) to warrant leadership at the executive level.

Even when this happens, considering the history, the HR function is forever doomed to be viewed as the expensive cost center mentioned earlier. It is considered a department that is tactically focused and generally on the defensive. The highest compliments that will ever be paid to the HR organization in companies that take this route are that it kept its expenses low and handled problems reasonably well.

The other path (and the one we heartily recommend) starts with the realization of the strategic importance of HR to the firm's success. The business plan will certainly address customer loyalty and will probably do it in quantitative terms. Enlightened leadership will perceive the direct link between HR strategies and customer loyalty, but, like anything else, it isn't going to happen by itself. Strategies must be developed and policies and processes set, all as an integral part of the company's strategies. An advocate is needed, and that advocate must be a member of the senior leadership team.

We are realists enough to know that high-growth companies cannot afford to hire senior executives willy-nilly. However, it costs nothing to formally acknowledge the obvious: *competent and motivated employees* are going to determine whether or not the company will acquire and retain customers, and ultimately determine whether or not the company will thrive or become a short-term, flash-in-the-pan success. And, it costs nothing for the "HR function" to become something more than an afterthought to whoever may oversee it, whether or not this person has an HR background.

The VSSCE Model

In the following section we present the *Vision/Mission*, *Strategies*, *Organizational Success Factors, Employee Competencies, Employees* (VSSCE) Model along with explanations and examples of how the model can and should work. For growth companies that choose to take the recommended path, the next chapter provides a road map with clear directions. It assumes that companies of any size can recognize the clear links among motivated employees, customer loyalty, and sustainable growth. It also assumes that growth companies will never have all the resources they might desire to establish and implement enlightened HR strategies.

But most important, it assumes that senior management *wants* to create sustained profitable growth through customer loyalty by fully developing and utilizing its most important asset, its employees.

THE VSSCE MODEL

VSSCE is a simple yet powerful way to look at the human resource function in your business, and it helps insure that all facets are properly oriented to provide maximum support of the company's customer-oriented mission and strategies.

In this section we present the model and describe both the reasoning behind it and how to apply it in practical terms. Properly aligning the "people" activities in your firm early on is another of those activities that, if accomplished early in the company's evolution, will help avoid the time-consuming and expensive "correction" later on. Without attempting to be smug, we firmly believe that your company will not sustain profitable growth without adopting the principles of VSSCE; it's simply a matter of whether you will do it sooner or later. Sooner is a lot less painful.

VSSCE

(Vision/Mission, Strategies, Organizational Success Factors, Employee Competencies, Employees)

Vision/Mission, Strategies

Every organization should define the reasons for its existence with clarity. Volumes have been written on the topic, and we will not repeat them here except to say that any ambiguity as to the sense of purpose of the firm will translate into escalating murkiness in its attempts to achieve it. As they say, without a clear sense of direction, any path will get you there. And, multiple paths will insure that you don't get anywhere.

Figure 7.1 VSSCE Model

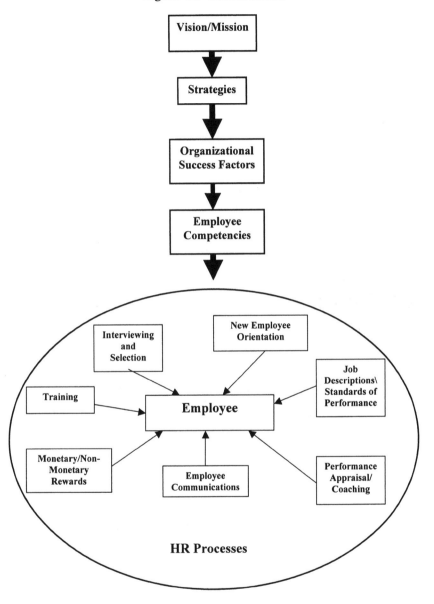

From the vision comes the strategies. We talked at length earlier as to the importance of insuring that the firm's strategies are kept current in light of marketplace changes, changes by the competitors, and changes within the company itself. With that accomplished, the company will have a defined set of courses of action required to achieve its vision.

Now the HR challenge begins. With a clear vision and well-defined strategies, how does the company insure that the behaviors of its employees, day in and day out, are supportive of and in sync with what the company wants to accomplish?

Organizational Success Factors

We define Organizational Success Factors as: Those few (usually no more than six to eight) goals or proficiencies in which the organization needs to excel in order to be successful as defined by its vision and strategies.

These, of course, vary from company to company, and every organization has its particular priority. When looking over the following list, the temptation is to conclude that almost every one is worthy of making the cut to become one of the top six to eight. However, it is imperative that you resist the urge to identify too many "number ones." The debate among senior management will be lively and productive, but fragmenting the emphasis among too many factors will dilute the effectiveness of the exercise.

Review the list; discuss, debate, and argue about the listings. Establish a consensus among team members and use the conclusions to specifically define exactly what your organization requires to become really proficient.

ORGANIZATIONAL SUCCESS FACTORS

Employee Competencies

We define Employee Competencies as: Those few (eight to ten) skills, abilities, types of knowledge, and judgment which, if possessed by the employees, will allow for superior job performance as measured against the company's Organizational Success Factors.

Simply put, what kind of behaviors do you need to satisfy the competency requirements?

Though the requirements will vary to some degree from one job to another, this exercise will help you define "our kind of person." We hear this phrase quite often, but most companies never define exactly what "our kind of person" really is nor do they institutionalize a process for insuring that the HR processes deliver "our kind of person." We use this term in its most positive context: the type person who possesses the skills, knowledge, and abilities that are aligned with the core competency requirements of the organization.

Table 7.1 Organization Success Factors

FACTOR Customer Satisfaction and Loyalty	INITIAL RANKING

Customer Satisfaction and Loyalty
- Enhanced Customer Satisfaction and Loyalty
- TQM and Continuous Improvement
- Customer Intelligence

Quality Products
- Enhanced Quality of Products
- Innovative/Customized Product Offerings
- Investment in Plant/Equipment
- Investment in Technology
- Enhanced Supplier Quality
- Brand Strength

Quality Service
- Enhanced Quality of Service
- Innovative/Customized Service Offerings

Business Processes
- Existing Process Improvement
- New/Innovative Processes
- Increased Manufacturing Efficiencies
- Increased Manufacturing Productivity
- Greater Asset Utilization

Employee Satisfaction and Development
- Leadership Development for Supervisors and Managers
- Job Skill/Competency Development for Non-Supervisory Employees
- Employee Retention
- Improved Employee/Organizational Communication
- Enhanced Employee Utilization/Productivity
- Enhanced Employee Satisfaction

Financial Performance
- Improved Financials [profit, margins, ROI, EBITDA, etc.]
- Growth in Sales and Market Share
- Competitive Pricing
- Cost Reduction
- Inventory Management/Turns

Table 7.1 (*Continued*)

FACTOR Customer Satisfaction and Loyalty	INITIAL RANKING
Acceptance of Innovation and Change • Greater Adaptability/Acceptance of Innovation and Change • Strategic Planning • Organizational Growth	

Following is a starter list of competencies. As with the Organizational Success Factors, the challenge here is to pare the list to those that are *really* critical to the company's ability to implement its strategies. We would all like every one of our employees to possess all the cited competencies, but, in reality, that isn't possible. So have another debate, and use the following list to define "our kind of person."

Competencies related to the Leadership of Others—Supervisors and Managers:

- Managing the Performance of Others: The ability to take responsibility for employees' performance by setting clear goals and expectations, tracking progress against the goals, providing feedback, and addressing performance problems and issues promptly.
- Developing Others' Capabilities: The ability to expand the capabilities and improve the performance of others through continuous coaching and mentoring.
- Empowering Others: The ability to convey confidence in employees' ability to be successful; delegating significant responsibility and authority; allowing employees the freedom to decide how they will accomplish their objectives.
- Fostering Teamwork: The ability to demonstrate interest, skill, and success in getting groups to learn to effectively work together.
- Establishing Focus: The ability to develop and communicate goals and strategies to others in support of the business's mission.
- Providing Motivational Support: The ability to enhance others' commitment and energy toward their work.

Competencies Related to Working with Others—Everyone:

- Teamwork/Cross-Functional Orientation: The ability to work cooperatively and effectively with others to achieve shared objectives; fosters collaboration and values the contribution of others.

- Building Collaborative Relationships: The ability to develop, maintain, and strengthen partnerships with others inside or outside the organization who can provide information, assistance, and support.
- Interpersonal Understanding/Empathy: The ability to anticipate, notice, and understand others' thoughts, concerns, and feelings and to communicate this awareness to them.
- Influence: The ability to be assertive in gaining others' support for proposals, projects, and solutions; leverages informal authority to mobilize others to action.
- Persuasive Communication: The ability to plan and deliver oral and written communication that makes an impact and persuades the intended audience.
- Oral Communication: The ability during conversations to clearly express oneself as well as discern messages from others.
- Written Communications: The ability to express oneself clearly in business writing.
- Attention to Communication: The ability to ensure that information is passed on to others who should be kept informed.

Competencies Related to Preventing and Solving Problems— Everyone:

- Strategic Thinking: The ability to analyze significant issues and the organization's position by considering issue-specific, corporate, marketplace, or industry implications.
- Technical/Functional Expertise: The ability to demonstrate a current depth of knowledge and/or skill in a technical, functional, and/or job-specific area.
- Diagnostic Information-Gathering: The ability to identify the information and sources needed to clarify a situation; not accepting "at face value," and using skillful questioning to draw out information.
- Forward Thinking: The ability to anticipate the implications and consequences of situations and take appropriate action to be prepared for the potential contingencies.
- Analytical Thinking: The ability to address an issue by breaking it apart and using a logical, systematic, sequential approach.
- Conceptual Thinking: The ability to address an issue by taking a holistic, abstract, or theoretical perspective.

Competencies Related to Achieving Results—Everyone:

- Customer Orientation: Continuously improving one's ability to identify and satisfy the needs of one's external and/or internal customers; develops effective working relationships with external and/or internal customers.

- Results and Execution Orientation: The ability to identify desired work results, establish and/or accept challenging goals, focus effort on those goals, and execute to closure; persists despite obstacles and opposition.

- Assuming Accountability for One's Performance/Career: Working with one's manager to clarify expectations, set goals, enlist needed support and feedback, prepare a personal development plan, and then personally take action to develop the skills needed in current and future jobs; takes responsibility for actions and outcomes.

- Operational Command of the Business: An understanding of the current issues relevant to the industry and organization; has and uses this cross-functional knowledge.

- Initiative: Identifying what needs to be done, assuming responsibility, and completing the task before being asked or before the situation requires it.

- Planning: The ability to put a project in perspective, determine the project's objectives, establish priorities, and allocate the resources necessary to accomplish the task.

- Quality Orientation: Ensuring that one's work is complete and accurate by carefully preparing, following up, and ensuring that all agreements and commitments have been fulfilled.

- Decisiveness: The ability to make difficult decisions in a timely manner.

- Fostering Innovation: The ability to develop, sponsor, and/or support the introduction of new and improved methods, products, services, and/or technologies.

- Resource Utilization: The ability to accomplish work requirements while optimizing the use of needed resources—capital, equipment, materials, facilities, and employees.

- Entrepreneurial Orientation: The ability to look for and seize profitable business opportunities; a willingness to take calculated risks to achieve business goals.

Competencies Related to Self-Management—Everyone:

- Priority-Setting and Time Management: The ability to allocate and appropriately use one's time to ensure that multiresponsibility deadlines are met.

- Adaptability: Openness to new ways of doing things and a willingness to modify one's preferred approach; demonstrating support for, initiating, and/or implementing the organizational changes necessary to improve the organization's effectiveness; working effectively in a variety of situations.

- Organizational Commitment: The ability to align one's behavior with the needs, priorities, and goals of the organization; putting the organization's objectives before one's own preferences or priorities.

- Personal Credibility: Exhibiting integrity and being perceived as responsible, reliable, and trustworthy.

- Self-Assurance: Faith in one's own ideas and capability to be successful; a willingness to take an independent position in the face of opposition.

- Stress Management and Self-Control: The ability to function effectively and control one's emotions in the face of pressure, hostility, and/or provocation.

The HR Processes

The VSSCE model culminates with the creation of a company's HR processes. Once the company defines its Organizational Success Factors and associated Employee Competencies, the HR processes must be developed, and, *most important*, they must be developed as an extension of the vision/strategy/success factors/competencies continuum, not as independent and isolated occurrences.

VSSCE illustrates the path we recommend in section 1 of this chapter. It requires a direct linkage between the company's vision/strategies and the HR processes. Anything else is unacceptable. As we detail the various HR functions in upcoming pages, we assume that you have customer loyalty as an integral part of your vision/strategy/success factors/competencies continuum. You may have others, but we believe strongly that customer loyalty will and should provide the overarching success factor that guides your HR process development.

We do not attempt to cover all the basic mechanics of each of the HR functions. Plenty of material exists that addresses the fundamentals. What we emphasize and provide are tools that will enhance each function's ability to acquire and retain competent and motivated employees... who will acquire and retain your customers.

To reiterate from section 1 again: *competent and motivated employees* are going to determine whether or not the company will acquire and retain customers, and ultimately determine whether or not the company will thrive or become a short-term, flash-in-the-pan success.

Interviewing and Selection

Four Seasons Hotel: Interviewed 17,000 people for 400 jobs for their New York Hotel.

Disney: Utilizes a "central casting" house and initial video, which culls 10 to 15 percent of initial applicants.

Nordstrom: "Hires nice people and teaches them to sell."

Peoples Jewelers: Identifies the common traits of their most successful employees and then recruits people who have similar traits.

Common sense tells us that the quality of the "raw material" in terms of employees brought into the firm is the foundation that insures that you have the employees required to insure customer loyalty. No matter the effectiveness of other HR processes, if an individual's basic personality traits and attitudes are not complementary with those requisite for the provision of high-quality customer service, the individual is likely to fail.

The practices of the premier service companies listed above illustrate several key elements that insure customer loyalty is pervasive in their interviewing and selection processes:

- You must have a large pool to select from.
- You must cull those who do not fit the desired model early on in the process.
- Some personality traits are more important than skills.
- You probably already know what you want if you look at your existing high performers.

Experience clearly indicates that the following competencies make for service quality:

- Tolerance for frustration.
- Dependability.
- Cooperative and a team player.
- Ability to work with various types of people.
- Able to work under pressure.
- Initiative and motivation.
- Communications skills, oral and written.
- Enthusiasm.
- Caring, full sense of ownership.

To obtain people with these competencies, we recommend that the following points become integral parts of your interviewing and selection process:

- Constantly increase the quantity and improve the quality of your candidate pool.
- Determine in advance the specific skills, knowledge, and traits required for each job.
- Utilize a structured, behavioral interviewing approach; build "ideal candidate competency profiles."
- Interview for service competencies (can do's) and inclination (will do's).

- Continually emphasize the significance of the customer and the company's service-oriented culture through the process.
- Utilize standardized, work-related simulations and role plays.
- Utilize personality testing to determine a service orientation.

New Employee Orientation

L.L.Bean: Two and a half hours dedicated to service on the first day on the job.

Nordstrom: First-day emphasis: "That's no problem; I can take care of that."

Disney: Minimum of two and a half days of customer service orientation.

Cracker Barrel: A video of the founder/chairman shown on the first day to emphasize quality service.

We challenge you to obtain the agenda your company currently utilizes in its new employee orientation programs. If we assume that service quality is a part of the agenda (and we hope it is), when is it covered relative to other topics, what percentage of time is devoted to it, and, how is it covered?

Our guess is that new employees will know more about how to fill out a claims form under the company's medical coverage than what the company thinks about service quality. Are the company's systems addressed before the reason they exist—to serve customers? And, do new employees find out about all the rules addressing what they *can't* do before they find out what they're *supposed* to do?

Companies rarely perceive just how much impact the first few hours or days on the payroll have on a new employee. Here we have energetic, motivated, and excited people who are virtual sponges. Their antennae are out, they're hanging on every word from their new employer. What a time for the company to make a lasting impression, an impression of what the company believes is most important. Is it an insurance form or serving the customer?

Now that you've reviewed your company's current orientation agenda and have decided it needs a little work, we urge you to address the following questions to insure that your company is giving its best first impression.

- Who's the audience?
- What do they know now?
- What message will they relate to?
- What message will have significance to them?
- What do they need to know and when?
- What's your company's service culture?

- What's your company's service strategy?
- What are the standards of performance for service?
- What are the reward and recognition systems when service excellence is delivered?
- How can you best convey the impact of service quality on customers, the company, and the company's ongoing well-being?
- What are new employees' most significant "moments of truth"? (Remember those?)
- What service skills/knowledge do they need to acquire?
- How can a quality service spirit be developed on day one?
- How can you convey the way the company wants its customers to be treated?

Remember, at this early stage with the company, new employees are "clean blackboards." Everything they see, hear, or sense will help form their view of what the company believes is important. This is a critical point in the game...don't fumble!

Job Descriptions/Standards of Performance

Ritz Carlton: Has a set of "Gold Standards," the "20 Basics" that every employee carries, one of which is reviewed daily in team meetings.

Herman Miller: Every day when employees turn on their computers, the first screen they see depicts the company's on-time shipment results from the day before and week to date.

McDonald's: Has twenty-six behavioral standards that employees are to follow when serving a customer.

Disney: Has different standards for treating excited, energized guests in the morning and fatigued guests in the afternoon.

An old adage declares that half the battle is just showing up. Perhaps analogous would be that half of insuring that employees do what you want them to do is to tell them what you want them to do. On the surface that may sound completely inane, but studies have indicated that only 40 percent of American employees know what performance requirements their supervisors have for them. Well, duh! How can they do *it* if they don't know what *it* is?

The development of specific and clearly communicated standards of performance is the obvious prerequisite for obtaining the desired behaviors. Those standards also form the basis of and support other behavior-impacting elements of the HR process:

- They establish and communicate the service quality theme.
- They reinforce the service quality philosophy.

- By definition, they establish specific, quantitative standards.
- They form the basis for training content.
- They are integral in the performance management process.
- They provide the basis for intervention and coaching.
- They form the basis of reward and recognition initiatives.

Next comes the formalization of that communication in terms of the job description, the institutionalized document that insures uniformity of expectations for all those performing like tasks.

Performance Appraisals/Coaching Though seemingly obvious, this is a critical link in driving service quality behaviors. To some degree, the success factors, general competencies, and even the job description can seem abstract to the individual employee. However, what is completely real are their individual performance appraisals, which are directly linked to monetary and nonmonetary rewards and recognition. And, it's a truism that what gets measured and rewarded gets done.

A direct linkage must exist between the performance standards established at the job description level and the actual expectations established for each individual. The standards are nothing more than theoretical if they don't become "up close and personal for each individual."

Then, if all these linkages are established, it's simply a matter of execution by the supervisor or manager. If the desired performance is not acknowledged and undesired performance not recognized and corrected, the best set of performance standards in the world are inconsequential.

Because the employee's morale (or lack of it) has direct consequences on the level of service, it is imperative that the administration of performance appraisals avoid several common and potentially disastrous pitfalls:

- The performance appraisal process is not a once-a-year "gotcha." Continuous dialogue between supervisor and employee all during the appraisal period (i.e., coaching) should insure that there are no surprises. The appraisal is not the time for an annual presentation of the year's failures or an annual heaping of praise. It should be a compilation and summarization of the pluses and minuses. Hopefully, praise has been bestowed and corrective action taken all during the year. If not, the employee has not received the motivation and development needed to maximize his performance.
- Supervisors do not "do" performance appraisals "to" employees. If the periodic performance appraisal is merely an extension of the continuing dialogue that should be going on between the two, it should be viewed by both as an opportunity for assessment, introspection, and moving forward.

- Performance feedback must be given against the backdrop of what the company is trying to accomplish in terms of its service to customers. Negative feedback regarding a service rep's lackadaisical attitude toward returning a customer's call within a designated time frame should be provided in the context of what it would mean to lose that customer ... not the fact that Rule 13.C.2 of the employee handbook had been broken.
- Poor communication skills on the part of the supervisor in providing feedback can have a demoralizing impact on employees. Even good news delivered the wrong way will be perceived as a negative. Care must be taken to insure that performance feedback is communicated appropriately, or the customer will ultimately suffer.

Effective coaching is the daily performance appraisal delivered by the employee's supervisor. In the simplest terms, a good coach:

- Lets employees know what's expected.
- Gives them the opportunity to perform.
- Tells them how they are performing.
- Provides assistance.
- Rewards them based on performance.

And, if enough positive motivators don't exist for every manager and supervisor to effectively coach their people, Mark McCormick summed up another reason rather succinctly: "You don't get fired by the person above you in the organization. You get fired by the people below you. The person above only gives you the message."

Monetary/Nonmonetary Rewards

Fed Ex: Any manager can grant a Bravo Zulu (well done) cash award to any employee exhibiting excellent service.

Cracker Barrel: Places stars on its employees' uniforms to recognize achievements.

Nordstrom: Has a merit pay plan for its sales staff that's 20 to 50 percent more than that of its competitors.

Disney: Rewards its outstanding employees with an assignment at Disney University for a year.

Chapters: Offers quarterly and annual pay incentives to employees in stores that achieve their profit objectives.

These leading service companies exemplify the creative use of both monetary and nonmonetary rewards. Each has a role, but both must be unequivocally tied to desired performance. What can possibly be worse than private or public awards being given to individuals who do not exemplify the best in service quality? What message is being sent to both the individual and other employees?

Monetary compensation schemes are diverse and as complicated or noncomplicated as the imagination can conceive. Every company should develop compensation plans that reward employees relative to the quality of service they provide customers, while meeting legal and regulatory requirements. But that's the easy part. What about nonmonetary rewards?

We have seen companies agonize more about relatively trivial nonmonetary rewards than their entire monetary compensation system...and they were probably right in doing so. As we said earlier, we're convinced that everyone thinks they know what everyone else is making, whether that assessment is accurate or not. But at least individual monetary compensation maintains the illusion of privacy. Not so nonmonetary rewards.

You may remember the hierarchy of employee motivators from the Maximizing Leadership Effectiveness chapter. Number one was "awareness and appreciation for their (employees) efforts." Number six was "compensation and benefits." Most nonmonetary rewards are very, very public. That's their nature. An employee is likely to become more excited about and interested in these rewards than with a perceived discrepancy of another individual's hourly wage.

We believe that nonmonetary rewards are powerful motivators. We also believe, however, that if they are not perceived as being "fair," or if they are rendered to those who exhibit behaviors inconsistent with the company's stated service quality strategies, they will absolutely cause more harm than good.

With that caveat, following is a list of nonmonetary rewards we believe are effective in a service-centric workplace. Note which ones your company utilizes...or should.

NON-MONETARY REWARDS

Table 7.2 Non-Monetary Rewards

REWARDS	DO/SHOULD YOU UTILIZE?
Recognition Meetings	
Seminar Attendance	
Special Parking Spaces	
Articles in Newsletter/Newspaper	
Notice on Bulletin Board	
Recognition at Employee Meetings	
Special Job Assignments	
Plaques	

Table 7.2 (*Continued*)

REWARDS	DO/SHOULD YOU UTILIZE?
Impromptu Meals/Snacks	
Handwritten Thank-You Notes	
Small Gifts…Coffee Mugs, Mousepads, etc.	
Charts/Posters with Service Results	
"Praising Coupons" issued to customers, who give them to employees for exceptional service and are redeemed for prizes	
Gift Certificates	
Sporting Event Tickets	
Recognition/Symbols on Employees' Name Badges	
Tuition Reimbursements	
Specialty Clothing	
Letters Sent to Employees' Homes	

Employee Communications If your company is serious about customers, you need to tell your employees about it…continually.

Though seemingly minor when compared to rewards and performance appraisals, employee communications should be the glue that ties all the components together. It is the company's public proclamation that customers have been important, are important, and will always be important.

However, the company must be committed to creating a consistent customer-focused message or run the risk of creating the impression among the employee base (not just the cynics) of a never-ending series of "causes du jour." One month it's customers. The next it's sales. The next it's safety. The next it's quality. Sure, sales, safety, and quality are important and deserve a place in employee communications, but there can be only one ongoing "most important" messaging theme. With the possible exception of a pure manufacturing environment, the overriding theme should focus on customers.

Communications channels are limited only by your imagination, but some of the most common include newsletters, meetings, e-mails, written memos, electronic/traditional bulletin boards, and company magazines. But the media selection is secondary to the creativity and consistency of the message.

An enterprising department head in a company with which we are familiar has a life-size dummy present at all his meetings. The dummy represents the customer, and the consistent message the manager delivers is "everything we say and do impacts our customers so lets not forget him [referring to the dummy]. He's here all the time."

The keys to successful employee communications programs seem to be the continuous repetition of the customer-focused message and "cheerleading" employee behaviors that exemplify the best in customer service quality.

Training

FedEx: Provides training and follow-through testing for forty thousand–plus carriers and customer service agents annually.

British Airways: Trains its thirty-seven thousand–plus customer service staff on "Communicating during Stressful Situations."

Ukrop's Grocery Stores: Offers "Healthy Start" (orientation), "Values," "Superior Customer Service," and "Teamwork" training courses to all its employees.

Mountain Co-Op: Requires a ten-day training course before employees interface with its members.

Disney: Cast members attend sixteen to forty-eight hours of training and must pass a test before interacting with a guest.

These examples from service quality leaders illustrate the commitment to training required by companies serious about service quality. Both new-hire training and ongoing refresher training are required to insure that employees are not only receiving the skill/ knowledge to do their jobs, but are also provided with continual reinforcement of the positive personal traits that were identified when they were hired.

However, although we are enthusiastic proponents of training, we urge caution and prudence when defining just what will be accomplished by training. How many times have we encountered a problem and said or heard, "Lets get some training for that"?

We urge executives, particularly when assessing training related to service quality, to be realistic in their expectations. When encountering service quality problems related to employee behaviors, one must look at the HR processes holistically to determine the source of the problem and its ultimate solution.

- If hiring standards don't exist, the best training in the industry will not produce satisfactory performers.
- If information systems are unsatisfactory and unreliable, no amount of "customer service training" will make up for the delays that customers experience.
- If the monetary rewards are not commensurate with those of a competitor across town, no amount of training will reduce employee churn, and thus customer churn.
- And, if the supervisors never provide feedback or coaching, you can't expect a trainer to deal with a year's worth of problems in two days.

So, training must be realistically assessed for what it can and cannot do. It can develop skills, convey knowledge, and enhance personal traits, but it cannot single-handedly compensate for deficiencies in other HR processes.

And, one last comment regarding training. In more companies than we care to recall, we've heard the following or something close to it directed to employees from the mouths of supervisors and managers: "Don't pay any attention to all that stuff they will told you in training. I'll show you how I want it done." Research clearly shows that the most important factor impacting how effective training will or will not be is the trainee's immediate supervisor.

Remember our proposition from an earlier chapter: Everyone pays more attention to their immediate supervisor than to anyone else in the company. There's no more effective way to negate the positive impact of training than for the trainee's supervisor to denigrate it.

SPECIAL CHALLENGES FOR GROWTH COMPANIES

If nothing else, we trust that the reader perceives a major message of this book . . . *the awareness of change and the need for it is required for successful growth.* From planning to execution to team interaction to culture, companies must incessantly reinvent everything to successfully navigate the stormy seas of change.

Change also has a tremendous impact on the employees of the company. Many if not most humans are naturally resistant to change. We all enjoy our comfort zones of stability, and given a choice would likely leave things just the way they are, assuming we are relatively content. If that assumption is accurate, senior management must realize the tremendous impact of continual change on employees. Though much of the focus so far has been on how the management team copes, everyone in the company is dealing with many of the same concerns. The senior team must recognize this and empathize with the employee body.

More on Vets and Recruits

This analogy was used previously in addressing teamwork issues within the senior management team and is equally relevant to employees as a whole.

The Vets It's highly probable that the veteran employees, those who have been with the company since the entrepreneurial stage, share the perspectives and outlook of senior managers with similar tenure. They all went through "basic training" together, have fought many battles alongside one another, and share a deep and personal loyalty to the company. They, like the veteran executives, were multitaskers, dealing with whatever had to be done at the moment regardless of their job title, department, or level in the organization. They also felt very close to the executives, working hand-in-hand with them every day. Many developed close personal and professional relationships with each other.

Veterans also perceive that they have a very strong work ethic ... and they probably do. When they were hired, the executives were personally involved in the selection process. Great care was taken in the early days to insure that every single new hire was top-rate; the company couldn't survive even a single weak link back then.

They have also personally observed the dramatic changes in the company, particularly the development of processes, procedures, chains of command, and hierarchy. They are familiar with the "good old days" and have a frame of reference for comparative opinions; whether they like the old or the new, they know the difference.

The Recruits The recruits are mostly a different breed. Without a historical frame of reference, the company is what it is. They don't know that the company was ever any different and don't really care. With the amount of hiring required for the rapid growth spurt, the company could not be as selective as it was during the entrepreneurial stage. Standards were not necessarily lowered, but, realistically, the company could not be as diligent as it was when the veterans were hired. As a group, the recruits have less loyalty to the company. They are all strangers to one another. When they joined the company, it had grown enough to offer more security than earlier. To many recruits, employment is "just a job." When the veterans joined, it was an adventure and a crusade.

The Potential Clash Though the vets and recruits are stereotypically presented, their differences in perspectives are vastly different. Melding these perspectives presents a challenge to management.

The Vets' Perspective

- "The company is lowering its standards."
- "These people would not have been hired two years ago."
- "The new employees are getting away with murder; we would have been fired if we had performed like they do."
- "All these damn processes and forms have been created to make sure the new employees don't screw up; I already know what to do and how to do it."

The Recruits' Perspective

- "The old-timers don't accept us."
- "The people that have been here a long time are too close to management; they've become 'company people.'"
- "They know a lot of stuff but don't help us like they should."
- "They know the executives too well and are obviously receiving favorable treatment."

Overburdening the Vets

Veteran employees represent a wealth of knowledge about how the company actually gets its work done daily. Before processes mature, a great deal of that knowledge resides in the veterans' heads. With rapid hiring it is critical that the senior team bridge the different outlooks of the vets and recruits to insure that this wisdom is shared. If the vets don't enthusiastically mentor the recruits, chaos results.

However, when the vets do "jump in," another problem presents itself. Literally, one morning the executives will come to work and discover that they have more recruits than vets. The implication is, they have more employees who don't know what they're doing than those who do. If the company is totally dependent on the vets conducting on-the-job training for all the new recruits, there's a high probability that the wheels are about to come off. The vets are so busy helping the recruits, they can't do their own jobs. Phones don't get answered, sales aren't made, and orders don't get entered...all sure ways to stop growth.

Senior management must be keenly aware of this dynamic and preempt it by implementing effective new employee orientation and training programs before it's too late. These programs must be in place *before* massive hiring begins. If they are not in place, it's one of those situations where you never seem to catch up.

Employees (and Information) You Can't Afford to Lose

Veteran employees carry many of the company's operating procedures in their heads. This is normal as companies grow and when few processes are in place. If all goes well, process and systems documentation proceeds; it captures and codifies vital data, and everything moves along swimmingly. Problems arise if or when an employee is in sole possession of critical information or knowledge and becomes discontented with the company or the company becomes discontented with the employee.

We are not referencing information that would be covered in non-compete or proprietary agreements. The critical data referred to here is information that may be of little use to a competitor, but is critical to the company. Primary examples include nondocumented or non-replicated:

- content originating in supplier negotiations
- production or fulfillment processes
- prospect/customer information
- software development
- systems restoration
- network configuration
- legal discussions

The prospect of losing or terminating an employee who possesses critical information presents a dilemma for the company:

- If the employee resigns the information is lost forever.
- In a termination scenario, attempting to capture the information will likely tip the employee off that he is in jeopardy, and cooperation is unlikely.
- The employee realizes the importance of the information and, subtlety or not so subtlety, blackmails the company.

Solutions to the dilemma are limited in number. But the company should take the following steps to insure that it doesn't put itself in an untenable position:

- Identify and prioritize information and knowledge that is critical to the company.
- Insure that the priorities are at the top of the process development/documentation list.
- Consider outsourced resources to expedite high-priority process development/documentation.
- Match up the high-priority issues with the individuals involved; determine the likelihood of the employee leaving the company at either party's insistence. Include this assessment in the overall priority analysis.
- Develop a "succession planning-like" process to insure that another individual becomes involved and begins to learn the subject matter, process, or design.

No matter what it takes, insure that the company does not put itself in a position of complete dependence on a single employee. The risks are very high, and no matter how positive the existing relationship, employees come and go. You really never know.

Management Layers

Not to spend much time covering ground that has been plowed many times, the first suggestion is: Don't have too many.

It is difficult to conceive of any situation where more than four management layers separate the task worker from the boss. In some industries or departments it might be less, but never more.

The rather standard structure:

- CEO/President/COO
- Officers
- Directors/Assistant VPs
- Managers/Specialists
- Supervisors/Specialists
- Task workers

Of more importance to growth companies is how the organization develops over time and who winds up where. Again, the focus is on change and how the employee base deals with it. Until the above structure or something similar evolves with growth, the company's organizational chart is very flat. In the entrepreneurial stage there were only two or three levels...the bosses, some more experienced task workers, and some lesser experienced task workers.

As time passed and the company grew, some veterans progressed and were promoted a level or two. Some stayed at the same level. Recruits filled all types of positions throughout the organization. The point: No company has the luxury of adopting what will be its ultimate organizational structure and filling the positions in an orderly manner. The structure and those who fill the slots are constantly in motion.

A growth company's organizational evolution is highly compressed in time. From creation to fairly mature business structure happens in a matter of a few years, not decades. Where any given employee resides relative to others on the organizational chart can change dramatically in a matter of months. Some peers from six months ago have advanced. Some may be at a lower level. This represents tremendous change for the individual.

As alluded to earlier, the perception that some employees are more equal than others in terms of their past relationships with senior management must not be perpetuated. Real or perceived informal channels of communication with senior management breed resentment and distrust. Friendships with employees throughout the company are to be cherished and respected. But senior management must be mindful not to allow friendship to become perceived as something it isn't.

The Hard Calls: Veterans That Have to Go

A simple matter of fact is, the company will outgrow the capabilities of some of the veterans. This will happen at all levels of the organization, not just with senior executives, and it poses some of the most gut-wrenching decisions the team will face.

Many of the veterans will make the required adjustments. They possess the talent and flexibility to change with the company. Some can't make the adjustment. They occupy positions where they were fully competent...a year and a half ago. But the requirements and demands of the job simply become more complex and demanding. As the job changes, they can't or won't.

More than likely, these veterans are solid employees and wonderful human beings. They were there at the beginning and worked like hell to make the company the success it is. They are intensely loyal and dedicated to the company and are doing the best they possibly can...but regrettably, it's not enough.

Stepping up to this issue is difficult for the management team. The natural inclination is to look for a similar-level position in the company for the individual. This option is not appropriate because all positions at that level require a similar level of capabilities and talent. It's unfair to both the individual and the company to shuffle employees from one position to another. The purpose of the company is not to preserve jobs.

It is likely that these employees will not be interested in a lower-level position. Therefore, termination remains the only option. The company owes a lot to veterans who find themselves in this situation and should take special care to insure that an appropriate severance package is provided. More important, the company should make every effort to preserve these employees' pride and self-esteem. These veterans were instrumental in getting the company to where it is today, and they deserve humane consideration.

People: What It's Really All About

In this chapter we have reviewed, almost from a clinical perspective, the implications of the HR organizational structure and many tools that will help insure that it is supportive of the company's growth objectives. However, what has been inferred but not overtly stated may be the most important message.

People are truly the heart and soul of any company, no matter its size, growth stage, or industry. This is not a revelation. Volumes have been written and scores of seminars and workshops presented that extol the importance of the human beings in the enterprise. We have touched on it several times in this book. And, there is no lack of public pronouncements by almost all companies as to the value of their employees. But, to use a well-worn cliché, common sense is not always common practice.

In these final paragraphs of the book, we will not attempt to delve into the subject in any level of detail . . . except to say that no company will prosper if it does not recognize and preserve the dignity of the people who work there. This is especially true of growth companies, which ask so much of their employees.

All the processes, compensation, motivation, and recognition schemes in the world are less than useless unless the firm's senior management team sincerely believes that the company's success is dependent on nothing more than the collective thoughts, actions, values, ethics, and talent of the employees.

They ARE the company. . .take care of them.

Conclusion

We began this book by offering sincere and deserved congratulations to those who have managed to successfully lead their companies through start-up . . . a period that presented unique challenges requiring courage, resourcefulness, and not a small amount of intestinal fortitude.

We trust that the reader realizes our appreciation of the tremendous efforts required for sheer survival at the beginning. However, it was our purpose in the book to honestly and forthrightly immerse you in the realities and challenges that come with the exhilaration of success. Forewarned is forearmed in many endeavors, and such is the case for a growth company. We have strived to provide those forewarnings that will assist you in preempting problems before they become detrimental to your company.

Once we "got your attention," we grouped our observations and suggestions around the Six Core Disciplines. It was a challenge for the authors to decide what to include and what didn't quite make the cut. However, after many hours of intense and at times rather heated discussion, we settled on the Six Core Disciplines presented herein. They represent the most critical points as determined by our research, experience, and discussion.

The complexity of the topics discussed ranges from the seemingly mundane to the overarchingly strategic. Sustaining profitable growth requires attention to the big things as well as the small. We hope we have come up with the optimum mix of both to ease your company's journey toward maturity.

We deliberately chose an informal presentation style for the material. Through the use of short paragraphs, bullet points, and self-assessment tools and other graphics, we desired to make the book an easy and quick read for busy businesspeople who appreciate brevity and conciseness.

Lastly, we sincerely hope this book has been helpful to you. We look forward to receiving any comments or input.

Good luck!

NOTES

INTRODUCTION

1. Larry Selden and Geoffrey Colvin, *Angel Customers & Demon Customers* (New York: Portfolio Books, Penguin Group, 2003).

2. Thomas K. Brown, "The Selling Trap," *Bank Director* 13, no. 3 (fourth quarter, 2003).

CHAPTER 1

1. W. Keith Schilit, *Rising Stars and Fast Fades* (New York: Lexington Books, 1994).

CHAPTER 2

1. Jill Griffin, *Customer Loyalty: How to Earn It and How to Keep It* (New York: Lexington Books, 1995).

2. Bradley T. Gale with Robert Chapman Wood, *Managing Customer Value: Creating Quality and Service that Customers Can See* (New York: Free Press, 1994).

3. Joan Koob Cannie, *Turning Lost Customers into Gold: The Art of Achieving Zero Defections* (New York: AMACOM, 1994).

4. Jan Carlzon, *Moments of Truth* (Cambridge, MA: Ballinger Publishing, 1987).

5. John Goodman. "Basic Facts on Customer Complaint Behavior and the Impact of Service on the Bottom Line." *Competitive Advantage*, June 1999.

CHAPTER 5

1. Stuart Levine, "Managing by Agreement: The New MBA," *Mediate.com*, April 2001.

CHAPTER 6

1. Larry Selden and Geoffrey Colvin, *Angel Customers & Demon Customers* (New York: Portfolio Books, Penguin Group, 2003).

2. Quoted in "The Customer Profitability Conundrum: When to Love 'Em or Leave 'Em", *Strategy + Business*, October 4, 2002.

3. Thomas K. Brown, "The Selling Trap," *Bank Director* 13, no. 3 (fourth quarter 2003).

4. Robert C. Docters, "Improving Profitability through Product Triage," *Business Horizons* (January–February 1996).

5. James B. Hangsteffer, *Creating and Sustaining Company Growth: An Entrepreneurial Perspective for Established Companies* (Waltham, MA: Burton-Merrill, 1997).

6. Tom Pryor, "The Demise of Gross Margin Pricing," *ICMS.net*

RESOURCES

ENHANCING CUSTOMER LOYALTY

Albrecht, Karl. *The Northbound Train: Finding the Purpose, Setting the Direction, Shaping the Destiny of Your Organization*. New York: AMACOM, 1994.

Barlow, Jannelle, and Claus Moller. *A Complaint Is a Gift: Using Customer Feedback as a Strategic Tool*. San Francisco: Berrett-Koehler, 1996.

Berry, Leonard L. *On Great Service: A Framework for Action*. New York: Free Press, 1995.

Cannie, Joan Koob. *Turning Lost Customers into Gold: The Art of Achieving Zero Defections*. New York: AMACOM, 1994.

Carlzon, Jan. *Moments of Truth*. Cambridge, MA: Ballinger Publishing, 1987.

Desatnick, Robert L. *Managing to Keep the Customer: How to Achieve and Maintain Superior Customer Service throughout the Organization*. San Francisco: Jossey-Bass Publishers, 1987.

Gale, Bradley T. *Managing Customer Value: Creating Quality and Service That Customers Can See*. New York: Free Press, 1994.

Griffin, Jill. *Customer Loyalty: How to Earn It and How to Keep It*. New York: Lexington Books, 1995.

Pine II, B. Joseph, and James H. Gilmore. *The Experience Economy*. Boston: Harvard Business School Press, 1999.

Reichheld, Frederick F. *Loyalty Rules! How Today's Leaders Build Lasting Relationships*. Boston: Harvard Business School Press, 2001.

Schneider, Benjamin, and David E. Bowen. *Winning the Service Game*. Boston: Harvard Business School Press, 1995.

Zeithaml, Valerie A., and Mary Jo Bitner. *Services Marketing: Integrating Customer Focus Across the Firm*. Boston: Irwin McGraw-Hill, 2000.

DYNAMIC PLANNING AND BUDGETING

Aaker, David A. *Developing Business Strategies*. New York: John Wiley & Sons, 1992.

Adizes, Ichak. *Corporate Lifecycles*. Englewood Cliffs, NJ: Prentice Hall, 1988.

Below, Patrick J., George L. Morrisey, and Betty L. Acomb. *The Executive Guide To Strategic Planning*. San Francisco: Jossey-Bass Publishers, 1987.

Coke, Al. *Seven Steps To a Successful Business Plan*. New York: AMACOM, 2002.

Kaplan, Robert S., and David P. Norton. *Translating Strategy into Action: The Balanced Scorecard*. Boston: Harvard Business School Press, 1996.

Kaplan, Robert S., and David P. Norton. *The Strategy-Focused Organization: How Balanced Scorecard Companies Thrive in the New Business Environment*. Boston: Harvard Business School Press, 2001.

Slywotzky, Adrian, and Richard Wise. *How to Grow When Markets Don't*. New York: Warner Business Books, 2003.

Zook, Chris. *Beyond the Core: Expand Your Market without Abandoning Your Roots*. Boston: Harvard Business School Press, 2004.

Zook, Chris, and James Allen. *Profit from the Core: Growth strategy in an Era of Turbulence*. Boston: Harvard Business School Press, 2001.

EXECUTING THE BUSINESS PLAN

Bossidy, Larry, and Ram Charan. *Execution: The Discipline of Getting Things Done*. New York: Crown Business, 2002.

Charan, Ram. *Profitable Growth Is Everyone's Business: 10 Tools You Can Use Monday Morning*. New York: Crown Press, 2004.

Fogg, C. Davis. *Team-Based Strategic Planning: A Complete Guide to Structuring, Facilitating, and Implementing the Process*. New York: AMACOM, 1994.

MAXIMIZING LEADERSHIP EFFECTIVENESS

Belasco, James A., and Ralph C. Stayer. *Flight of the Buffalo: Soaring To Excellence, Learning to Let Employees Lead*. New York: Warner Books, 1993.

Buckingham, Marcus, and Curt Coffman. *First, Break All The Rules*. New York: Simon & Schuster, 1999.

Collins, Jim. *Good To Great: Why Some Companies Make the Leap . . . and Others Don't*. New York: HarperCollins Publishers, 2001.

Giuliani, Rudolph W. *Leadership*. New York: Talk Miramax Books, 2002.

Kotter, James P., and James L. Heskett. *Corporate Culture and Performance*. New York: Free Press, 1992.

Kouzes, James M., and Barry Z. Posner. *The Leadership Challenge: How to Keep Getting Extraordinary Things Done in Organizations*. San Francisco: Jossey-Bass Publishers, 1995.

Mackoff, Barbara, and Gary Wenet. *The Inner Working of Leaders: Leadership as a Habit of Mind*. New York: AMACOM, 2001.

Maxwell, John. *The 21 Indispensable Qualities of a Leader: Becoming the Person Others Will Want to Follow*. Nashville: Thomas Nelson Publishers, 1999.

CHANGING EMPHASIS FROM SALES/REVENUE TO MARGIN/PROFITS

Berends, William. *Price & Profit: The Essential Guide To Product & Service Pricing and Profit Forecasting*. Oakville, Ontario: Berends & Associates, 2004.

Lee, Bill. *Gross Margin: 26 Factors Affecting Your Bottom Line*. New Oxford, 2003.

Lenskold, James D. *Marketing ROI: The Path To Campaign, Customer, and Corporate Profitability*. New York: McGraw-Hill, 2003.

Robert C. Docters, "Improving Profitability through Product Triage," *Business Horizons* (January–February 1996).

Selden, Larry, and Geoffrey Colvin. *Angel Customers & Devil Customers*. New York: Penguin Group, 2003.

Quoted in "The Customer Profitability Conundrum: When to Love 'Em or Leave 'Em", *Strategy + Business*, October 4, 2002.

POSITIONING HR MANAGEMENT AS A STRATEGIC ADVANTAGE

Connellan, Tom. *Inside the Magic Kingdom: Seven Keys To Disney's Success*. Austin: Bard Press, 1996.

Disney Institute. *Be Our Guest: Perfecting the Art of Customer Service*. New York: Disney Editions, 2001.

Dubois, David D., and William J. Rothwell. *Competency-Based Human Resource Management*. Palo Alto: Davies-Black Publishing, 2004.

Lucia, Anntinette D., and Richard Lepsinger. *The Art and Science of Competency Models: Pinpointing Critical Success Factors in Organizations*. San Francisco: Jossey-Bass/Pfeiffer, 1999.

Rosenbluth, Hal F., and Diane McFerrin Peters. *The Customer Comes Second and Other Secrets of Exceptional Service*. New York: William Morrow, 1992.

Spencer, Jr., PhD, Lyle M., and Signe M. Spencer. *Competence at Work: Models for Superior Performance*. New York: John Wiley & Sons, 1993.

Ulrich, David. "Delivering Results: A New Mandate for the Human Resource Professional," Boston: Harvard Business Review, 1998.

GENERAL

Brown, Thomas K. "The Selling Trap," *Bank Director* 13, no. 3 (fourth quarter, 2003).

Schilit, W. Keith. *Rising Stars and Fast Fades*. New York: Lexington Books, 1994.

INDEX

ABOUT THE AUTHORS

THE FOCUS GROUP

Rodney Page and Pete Tosh formed The Focus Group in 2004 with the express purpose of utilizing their collective experience to help senior management of growth-oriented companies realize their potential—by achieving, managing, and sustaining profitable growth. Multiple resources are available to start-up firms and mature companies, but we strongly believe that the challenges faced by high-growth early-stage companies that are between those extremes have been long ignored. The Focus Group and this book are efforts to insure that the emerging companies of today maximize the opportunities before them and become the stars of tomorrow.

RODNEY PAGE

Rodney has worked for and with many organizations during his thirty-four-plus years in business, primarily focused on general management and sales/marketing. A native of Macon, Georgia, Rodney is a graduate of the University of Georgia, where he majored in Advertising/Marketing. After twenty-one years with a *Fortune* 500 telecommunications firm, Rodney participated in several entrepreneurial ventures, including establishing his own consulting firm. Rodney currently splits his time between Macon and St Simons Island, GA.

PETE TOSH

After studying psychology, industrial psychology, and business, Pete had fifteen years of extensive corporate experience in the chemical, aluminum, and health care industries within the functional areas of human resources and quality. As a management consultant for twenty years, Pete has assisted organizations around the world to maximize customer loyalty through the implementation "best practice" human resource and customer satisfaction practices. Pete lives with his wife Katy and their Labrador retriever, Madison, in Macon, Georgia.

Rodney and Pete can be contacted at The Focus Group:
577 Mulberry Street
Suite 1015
Macon, Georgia 31201
(478) 746 6891
www.thefocusgroup.biz